The Power of CONNECTION PROJECT

Andrea Rosenzweig

Paperback ISBN: 978-1-945587-61-0
Hardback ISBN 978-1-945587-60-3
Library of Congress Control Number: 2020920901
Andrea Rosenzweig
The Power of Connection Project
1. Self help; 2. Homelessness; 3. Humanitarianism; 4. Philanthropy

Cover Design: Brittney Gaddis
Cover Photo: Kimberly Teichrow
Typesetting and Design: Dancing Moon Press

Dancing Moon Press
Bend, Oregon USA
dancingmoonpress.com

For more information and to order bracelets, see andrearosenzweig.com

DANCING
MOON
PRESS

Dedication

"By actively seeking ways to connect to those who need us most, we find our connection to ourselves." — Andrea Rosenzweig

Thanks to all who love me and who have allowed me to love them.

Thanks to brave humans everywhere who dare to ask for help.

Love does make the world go round.

Introduction

Have you ever felt lonely?

Disconnected?

Running through the motions?

Checked out?

A few years ago, I had reached a point in my life where I was feeling stuck. My life, with its ups and downs and twists and turns, included a happy marriage to my high school sweetheart that took us from Georgia to Oregon. In the Pacific Northwest, we fell knee-deep into raising four kids and running a small business. Throw in losing a parent, health challenges, and teenagers and there is no surprise why I was struggling. I arrived at a season of life where I needed a reboot, a fresh start, and something to jolt me into the practice of finding joy in the present moment again. I wanted nothing more than to focus on the positive and find gratitude for all the good in my life, but I felt like I was treading water.

The awareness of my season of discontent came the same year I took a life-changing trip to Kenya. On the trip, I was privileged to spend time with the Maasai people in a remote village in the Transmara. They brought me into their circle and allowed me to experience their simple, communal, and joyful life—a life that revolved around connection with their culture and community, reverence for education, and a connection to their land.

The Maasai women, in particular, welcomed me into their homes and showered me with love and connection, even though I was a stranger to them. These women were the embodiment of love. They took a handmade bracelet off their arm and placed it onto mine, complete with a hug. It was a simple, kind gesture, that to this day reminds me of feeling connected and cared for.

In Kenya, the government does not pay for girls to receive education past middle school. This leads many down a path of early pregnancy with little to no job skills for future success. The grandmothers and mothers sit together all day, making these beaded bracelets, in the hopes that they can sell them to help pay for school fees for their daughters and granddaughters. The women are doing what they can to empower and support these young women, to give them a chance at a future.

I came home from that trip and felt inspired. The women sent me home with 400 bracelets, hoping I could help their efforts when I returned to the US. I had to come up with a plan. I personally decided that in lieu of Christmas presents for our family, I would purchase 24 bracelets, which would send two girls to school for the year.

Now I had to decide what to do with the remainder of the bracelets. I thought back to my own desire to escape the lonely rut I was in. To me, the opposite of loneliness is connection. I decided to challenge myself to connect with someone in my daily life who may be hurting, lost, or need a little love each of the 24 days leading up to Christmas. I would connect with them, offer my help, and gift them with a bracelet made by the same Kenyan women I met on my travels. I hoped to remind myself and those I met along the way about the power of connection and community. The power of friendship. The power of seeing someone and letting them know they matter. The power of feeling connected and cared for.

Unknowingly, this new idea started me on the greatest and most important challenge I have ever been on—one that I have now turned into an annual tradition. When we are connected, we feel more grounded in ourselves. The stories that follow in these pages of the people I've connected with and what happened when we encountered one another have inspired thousands of people to connect, purchase bracelets, and send Kenyan girls to school.

My wish is for everyone to experience the Power of Connection Challenge and to find the inspiration they need to reach out to someone and find out what they need most. True connection creates a powerful ripple effect impacting communities across the globe, across households, across hearts—and even across rural Kenyan villages.

Along with the stories of connection and daily inspirational messages in this book, you will find a link to purchase a Kenyan handmade bracelet.

May you find a way to gift it to someone who you feel needs love and connection.

What a perfect gift we can give to the world and to each other.

We are all stronger, together.

"It is not how much we give, but how much love we put into giving." —Mother Teresa

Day 1

VETERANS

Glen was out of gas and holding a sign asking for help in our local Walmart parking lot. His truck was covered in stickers depicting his military service. As I approached him, I noticed his Vietnam veteran hat. We struck up a conversation and I listened as he recounted his current situation. After hearing about his setbacks, I offered to buy him a tank of gas. He was appreciative. Then I explained that I had one more thing to give him: a friendship bracelet made by women in Kenya trying to send the girls in their community to school.

I explained what it had meant to me and what I hoped it would mean for Glen. Glen was moved. As I placed the bracelet on his wrist, he immediately began to tell me about his faith in God, his desire as a young boy to become a minister, his struggles with depression when he entered the service, how he earned two Purple Hearts but came home to be spit on by protesters, and how he found his faith again and is helping other vets today. What an honor it was to hear his story. Thank you, Glen!

Message of the day

Every veteran deserves to tell their story and be heard. Can you find a veteran today, listen to their story, and show your appreciation?

Day 2

OLDER, WISER CROWD

Rachel-
What a wonderful and positive experience it has been meeting you.
Your gift of the bracelet is one I can enjoy every day. I love the color.
I look forward to the time when your mom and you come to Touchmark. Hopefully that will be soon.

My daughter Rachel spent time at school interviewing a resident at a local retirement home for a biography project. She was paired with Lois, and Rachel did a great job asking questions, listening and documenting Lois's life. "Come any time!" Lois told us, and handed Rachel her number on a piece of paper.

Rachel enjoyed her time with Lois so much that we try and visit her for tea-time whenever we can. Lois loves her time with Rachel and she LOVES her bracelet. She doesn't have family in town, so her bracelet reminds her of our connection throughout the holidays and beyond.

Lois wrote and mailed a thank-you note the SAME day she received the bracelet. This is how the older, wiser crowd rolls, and it was inspiring. There is so much to learn from the OWC (older, wiser crowd). They have so much perspective to share about life, their childhood stories are colorful and fascinating to kids (and adults!), and their poise and respectful communication skills are warm and genuine reminders of how we can aspire to live simply within our technology-centered and sometimes impersonal and disconnected world.

Message of the day

Who can you write a thank-you card to today?

Day 3

LOVE YOUR NEIGHBOR

During a crazy snowstorm that forced school closings, I decided to try visiting my neighbor. You see, we have lived in our home for 11 years. In 11 years, we have never met our next-door neighbor. The neighbors on the other side of our house are good friends. They are retirees who have my kids over for graham crackers with butter and chocolate milk. My husband and my neighbor go on fishing trips together. They are like family. We stand outside and talk about life, and I know I can call them in an emergency.

I am embarrassed to admit it, but the neighbor on the other side is simply referred to by our kids as "the old lady." When we moved in, I was pregnant with Rachel and had two toddlers. Life was busy. Rarely, I would catch a glimpse of her peering over at our home, startled by one of the many crazy noises coming from our house. We would see her in her driveway in the summer, taking a brief walk for fresh air. Sometimes, we would wave to her, hoping for an invitation to introduce ourselves. However, she always looked puzzled, looked away, or walked back towards her home. She mostly stayed inside. As the years ticked by, another baby came, new puppies, friends, basketball games in the driveway, bike-riding lessons, and all of the chaotic fullness that comes with a decade of raising four kids.

Eventually when we would see her, we didn't really take notice. She became part of the background of life.

Until this advent challenge.

Originally, I planned to visit her on Christmas Eve, the final day of the challenge. I imagined taking cookies over to her, introducing ourselves, and wishing her a Merry Christmas. We would all be so happy to have finally met and we would be instant friends. But that was just my imagination talking.

I have been to her house four times now during this challenge, but she won't open the door. At first, we thought maybe she thought we were selling something. So we tried again. And again. And again. One day I saw her in the window and waved as I approached before she disappeared around the corner. That time we left a note explaining we were her neighbors, wrote down my phone number, and included a bracelet. Today I was determined. "It is cold and snowy," I explained to my husband. "The boys could bring her wood or shovel her driveway!" My own mom who lives alone has many neighbors helping her every day to get through this weather.

Rachel and I trudged through the knee-deep snow. We were the only footprints in her driveway. We knocked. We rang the bell. "I want to help her, Mom," Rachel said. "I want her to know we care." There was no answer. I felt ashamed.

Why did I waste so much time? It's amazing in our lives how busy we get. How many times I had the opportunity to run over and strike up a conversation that put us both at ease. How our lives are so isolated now that we don't even know our neighbors. We are so self-focused on our own families.

When we went to the door today, my phone number and bracelet were gone. I can at least rest in knowing that while we might not eat cookies by the fire and be fast friends, she does know we care. She does have our number in case of an emergency, and the next time we see her walking down the driveway in the summer air, you can bet I will be jogging over to say hello in person and explain why a Kenyan bracelet was on her doorstep.

Message of the day

Go meet a neighbor you don't know yet!

Day 4

A GIFT THAT MATTERS

My daughter and I cleaned and organized her room, where I found quite a few items that we purchased during our back-to-school shopping that still had the tags on them. Her style had changed in the few months since we shopped, and by then she only preferred sports clothes (go figure). I made a small pile and told myself to make the returns during my errands that week.

I parked at the shopping center and I saw a man on the corner across the street. I walked over to where I could read his sign, and it read "Happy Holidays." I smiled to myself, thinking that, of all the signs I have seen, this is the first one that mentioned the holiday season and nothing else. I locked my car and walked over to him.

"Hi," I said. "What do you need most right now?"

He was a handsome guy, bundled up in the 20-degree weather. "Thank you for asking," he said. "I really need batteries most."

"Batteries?" I questioned, "What type of batteries?" He told me AAA and AA batteries would be really helpful.

I looked around at the shopping center I was standing in. Dick's Sporting Goods store was right behind me. I knew that I had an item in my return pile in the car that might help towards this battery request. "Okay," I told him, "I will be right back with batteries."

I walked back to my car and took out the item to return. I had purchased it late in the summer and I wondered if they would take it this much later for a return. As I approached the store, I noticed the store windows at Dick's. It said, "GIVE A GIFT THAT MATTERS."

What an epiphany I had standing there at that moment. I was returning a gift we hadn't really needed—for a gift that MATTERED! I walked through the doors and an associate led me back to the batteries. I picked up four packages of batteries and headed to the cashier.

At the checkout, they took back my return item and applied the credit towards the purchase. They even gave me 25% off the batteries. I headed back out to my new friend and he met me in the parking lot.

He looked in the bag and dug around in surprise. "Thank you SO much!" he said. I asked if he was living outside in this weather and he nodded. "My wife and I live at an outdoor homeless camp, and these batteries will help us run our flashlights, radios, and battery heaters."

I introduced myself and learned that my new friend's name was Brett. I offered him a bracelet and explained its meaning. He looked at it, and just as I thought he was going to say that he would give it to his wife, he said, "I am going to give it to my sister. She brings us food each week and I can never get her a present—she will love this."

A gift that MATTERS! Brett wants to give his sister a gift that matters. Maybe this Christmas we can ask our kids (and each other!) to focus on gifts that matter.

Message of the day

Do you have something unused that you could return and purchase a gift that matters?

Day 5

HUG A KID TODAY

My son Tyler and I were driving when the snow turned to rain and it began to come down heavily. We spotted someone on a street corner holding a sign. As we got closer, Tyler told me the sign said, "trying to stay warm." Tyler suggested, "Let's get him a Starbucks card so he can get warm drinks," pointing to the Starbucks across the street from the corner. "That might be good," I said. I quickly turned into the parking lot, parked, and walked over.

As I got closer, I realized the "person" was actually a teenager, with the same straggly mustache hairs my own boys are beginning to grow. As we approached him, his dog barked ferociously at me, and he told her to behave. "I saw that your sign said that you are trying to stay warm, so what do you need most right now?" I asked him. He replied, "Actually ma'am, I could really use a tent." My heart stopped for a moment. "Are you sleeping outside in this weather?" I asked. "Yes," he replied. "Are you able to stay warm enough in a tent in this weather?" My mama bear instincts started kicking in. "I have lots of blankets," he told me, "so I stay pretty warm. It's just that last night, the temperatures got so low that my zipper froze, and when I pulled it closed, all the plastic parts of the zipper came off—and now it won't close at all," he said.

"I will go get you a tent," I decided. "What type of tent is best?" I asked, and as he told me what he needed I scanned the shopping centers around us. "I am not sure anywhere around here will have a tent," I said out loud. He mentioned Costco, and I said I would go try and be right back. "That's really kind of you," he said. He told me his name was Zach, and he reached out to shake my hand.

Tyler and I rushed over to Costco, which happened to be in the same shopping center. As I went up and down every aisle, all I saw were toys and more toys. Video games, keyboards, giant teddy bears, LEGO sets...I began to get frustrated. Where are the tents? I need to get a boy a tent, so he can sleep safely in the snow! I grabbed a Costco employee who laughed loudly—"A TENT? We don't sell tents in the winter!" I was getting angry and desperate. Where would I find a tent for Zach and his dog? How long would he wait there?

Tyler and I ran out of Costco and back to the car. We drove back to Zach and explained that we had to drive to the sporting goods store to find a tent. I asked him if he wanted to wait somewhere warm while we were gone, but he told us, "That's okay, it's not raining that bad."

We drove over to the sporting goods store and walked in. The store had tents! I tried to determine which one would keep him warm, grabbed the best choice, ran to the checkout, and then to the car.

Tyler and I raced back across town with our tent and prayed that Zach had not given up on us. We saw him, soaked, but still standing there on the corner. We parked and got out. We handed Zach the tent and asked if it would work. "It's perfect," he said. Then he asked if he could give Tyler and me both a hug. We gave him a hug, but the mom in me couldn't leave him. "How long have you…" I struggled to find the words. "Lived outside?" he finished. "Two years now."

I gave him a bracelet and explained its significance. He said it was a beautiful bracelet. I asked him to tell us something about himself, and he said that he likes rock 'n' roll, and that he named his dog Andromeda because he thought her spots looked like stars. I asked if he would take a picture with me, but he stiffened up, and his mood changed instantly. "No ma'am—absolutely no pictures, please." I immediately understood. I asked if he would like my waterproof ski gloves in the car and he said, "Yes, please. I would like that very much." We exchanged goodbyes and wished him well. We got back in the car and drove out of the parking lot. Tyler and I watched him cross the road and head for the woods.

Zach is someone's polite, kind, teenager—and he is sleeping in the woods tonight.

Message of the day

Hug your kids today and tell them you love them. Hug someone else's kid and tell them how amazing they are. Let's love on all the kids we see today and every day, in schools, on sports teams and on street corners.

Day 6

THE GIFT OF CONNECTION

Yesterday, when I ran into Safeway, the cashier ringing me up noticed my bracelet and commented that she thought it was beautiful. She asked where it was from and I told her it was given to me by women in Kenya. "You went to Africa?" she perked up in interest. I told her about my trip and what the bracelet symbolized for me—and then the exchange was over. As I headed home, I decided that I would get another bracelet and take it back to her. I looked at my receipt and learned that her name was Pamela.

By the time I returned with the bracelet, the store manager told me Pamela was gone for the day, but she would be back from 8-12 tomorrow.

So early the next morning I walked into Safeway and right up to Pamela. I said, "You were my cashier yesterday." She looked worried. Then I pointed to my bracelet and said, "You mentioned that you liked my bracelet." Her eyes got really big. "So, I came back today to give you one." I reached into my pocket and she literally gasped. "Oh my gosh, oh my gosh, oh my gosh," she cried. "My favorite color is green, oh I'm so excited, oh I can't believe it." She started crying, right there on the spot. She asked me for a hug. The bracelet was small, so we spent a few minutes stretching it and finally got it on—she was determined. We hugged off and on for a good, solid five minutes, as shoppers went through her line checking out. Each person would get a "look at my beautiful bracelet, isn't it just beautiful?" as she showed them her new gift.

When we were alone again, Pamela told me, "I live alone. And I don't do Christmas really well. In fact—I don't really even do Christmas. This [pointing to the bracelet]—this is MY Christmas. This is MY joy." She asked for my information so that when shoppers liked her bracelet she could direct them to me to sell more and help the village girls with their school fees. "I am going to sell a lot of bracelets for you," she said.

Then she asked if she could shower with her bracelet on, which made me smile, knowing she doesn't ever want to take it off.

Message of the day

Can you strike up a conversation with someone today during a routine errand and let them know that they matter and that you care?

Day 7

MOMS

It was 28 degrees when I saw a bundled woman with a sign that read "Mom in need—anything helps." I rolled down the window and asked her what she needed most. She told me size 4 diapers and wipes. I told her I would run to the store and be right back.

I grabbed a box of diapers and some wipes and thought about her baby. The baby on the Huggies box looked so happy and cute, I noticed as I waited to check out. "Where is her baby right now as she waits in the cold?" I wondered.

I drove back and got out of the car. I handed her the diapers and wipes, and she told me times were really hard. She said her name was Laura, and that her 20-month-old baby's name was Jamie. "Best thing that ever happened to me," she stated. She and her husband were renting a hotel room which cost $60 a night. He worked the graveyard shift and was home with the baby right now while she looked for some help. They were just barely getting by.

I gave her a bracelet and explained its meaning. I told her to remember that people care about her. She told me that she had just lost her mother that past May at only 65 years old. She missed her. "Guess what?" she said in a loud, happy voice that startled me after our somber conversation. "Guess when my mom's birthday is!"

"Today?" I asked.

"No—December 25," she said with a big smile. "Things are looking up!" she exclaimed.

And with that, we parted, and I wished her a Merry Christmas and a Happy Birthday to her mom.

Moms standing in the cold for diapers, moms supporting moms, moms remembering and missing their moms. This was a reminder the world needs and loves our MOMS.

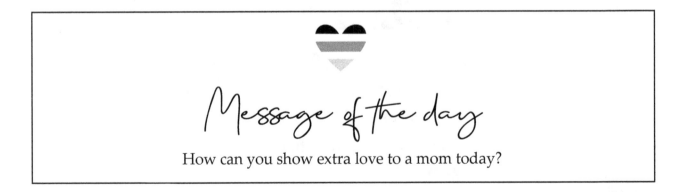

Message of the day

How can you show extra love to a mom today?

Day 8

LOVE IS THE UNIVERSAL LANGUAGE

All day today, it hovered around 32 degrees, and we saw some rain and snow. My daughter and I decided we would buy a large hot chocolate and gift it with a bracelet to a person who could use some warmth. As we drove away with hot chocolate in hand, we spotted a man pushing his bike (with his trailer of belongings) quickly down the sidewalk. We both agreed he was the one who needed our warm treat, so we parked and got out to meet our new friend.

As soon as he saw us, he stopped his bike and waited for an explanation. I offered him the hot chocolate and he quickly placed it in his bike's cup holder. Then I reached in my pocket and told him, "I also have a bracelet for you." I pointed to mine, and he looked puzzled. At this point, he opened his mouth to speak, but no words came out. Suddenly, it was clear this man did not have the ability to speak. He rolled up the sleeves of his many warm layers until his wrist was exposed. I snapped the bracelet on and he immediately began to try frantically to communicate with my daughter and me.

He wrote out his name on his palm, tracing with his fingers: B-O-B. He made a lot of hand gestures about airplanes, sticking his arms out as if he was flying, and he motioned that he flew a far distance by pointing far away. After trying to motion and mouth a few things, we were not understanding him easily, so he pulled off both sets of gloves and pulled out a phone. He opened an app and pulled up a map of the Philippines. Bacolod, Philippines came up, and he kept pointing—frantically. Yes, we nodded, we see your map, we see.

Then he opened a weather app, and he showed us the weather forecast for Bend: all week, snow and frigid temperatures. He made a disgruntled face. Yes, we understand, we chuckled. Then he quickly opened up Bacolod, Philippines on the weather app. 80 degrees and sunny there all week. He pointed and looked in my eyes: this is where he wanted to be today. His eyes just sparkled. He even gestured to wearing shorts—bless his heart! I could relate; Bacolod sounded great on a freezing cold day like today!

Then he opened his pictures—and suddenly I realized the real reason Bob wanted to be in Bacolod. He scrolled through picture after picture of him with his love in Bacolod. He pointed and stared longingly at each one. Bob looked handsome and happy, each picture showing the two of them in a warm embrace or kiss. He wanted me to see her, even zoomed in on her face on each one. It was apparent that she is his world. He smiled, patted his heart, even pointed to his ring finger. He loves this woman. Again, he made the motion of the airplane flying to her.

I told Bob that we were glad to meet him. He smiled and told us "thank you" in sign language. I said Merry Christmas and Bob mouthed that his birthday is December 23rd. Rachel and I wished him a Happy (early) Birthday. He smiled and we parted.

As he pushed his bike down the sidewalk once more, Rachel and I got back in the car. Neither of us could let go of wondering where Bob was tonight and if he was warm. I knew he would dream of being on a warm beach with someone he loves when he went to sleep. I hoped his bracelet would remind him that two people in Bend heard his love story, that we cared about him, and we both hoped he would be reunited with his love again someday in Bacolod.

Message of the day

Ask someone to tell you about their love story.

Day 9

TEACH

"He who learns, teaches." —Ethiopian proverb

Teaching is in my family. My parents met as teachers, my mom spent her career as a teacher and counselor, and I became a teacher, too.

I chose to teach because I love education and I wanted to make a difference in a young person's life. I didn't spend many years teaching before I had kids of my own, but I still look back at those years as some of the best in my life.

Teachers spend more waking hours with our kids on a daily basis than we parents do. Their voices can shape our children's view of education and their self-esteem.

Teachers, with families and struggles of their own, come in to work and care for kids. They love them, encourage them, have compassion for them, and keep pushing them to be their best selves. Teachers inspire, engage, and encourage kids to stay curious about life.

I was an easy student; I followed the rules, was diligent, and loved my teachers. I fit into the education system, and I loved school.

My husband, as a young student, was quite the opposite. The stories he tells of school antics, with trouble and more trouble, led me to believe that he was quite the pain in every teacher's behind. Yet when he went back to a reunion years later, I was shocked to hear all of the loving things his former teachers had to say about him. "You and your friends were so great," "We loved you boys so much," "You were fun and a great kid." I asked my husband how his teachers could remember things in such a positive light after all the trouble he had been in. "My teachers always loved me," he said with a grin.

Good teachers see each kid as an individual. My four children couldn't be more different in the education world. Some are easy students and some are hard. Some please and some distract. Some are disorganized and some are achievers. Some are anxious and some have learning disabilities. But each day they head to school, a teacher has a chance to love them. They have the chance to see them—not for their weaknesses, but for their potential. And for the kids that are hard to teach—love them harder. Trust me, these kids are seeing just how far you are willing to walk with them and how soon you will give up. Please don't give up—try to laugh more, connect more, praise more, forgive more, and believe in them more. They need you twice as much to get through school.

Please, teachers—please remember the incredible influence that you have on each and every one of your students. You probably became a teacher for the same reasons I did: to make a difference. YOU MATTER. You set the tone for how students treat each other by how you treat them and how they view learning. You have the chance to demonstrate love and compassion to every student you teach—students who may not get those experiences anywhere else. You may be the one who can help a student feel less alone and discouraged, and to have hope.

Hopefully one day a pain-in-the-behind student will come back and tell YOU, "Thanks for putting up with me, laughing with me, believing in me and loving me."

And he who learns love—teaches love.

Message of the day

Remember someone who has taught you a valuable lesson and show them some love.

Day 10

FOOD IS LOVE

Sometimes we all go through difficult seasons. During these times, we expend most of our energy on the daily survival tasks while also sorting through our emotions. Deaths, illnesses, and holidays are all times when food can be used as healing or celebration.

So after a particularly trying week (which no one really knew about), I arrived home and saw that my friend Elizabeth had surprised me and dropped off a full meal of homemade tamales, rice, and salsa. My heart melted at this surprise gift offering. I felt instant joy, love, connection, and relief.

If you ever wonder whether you should make someone a meal during a hard time, during the holidays, or for no reason at all—DO IT.

A gift of homemade food is the ultimate gift of love. It is also a dying art. We are all so busy simply trying to actually feed our own families that taking the time to plan and prepare something for someone else takes intentional effort, time, and love. However, it also connects and fulfills us to nourish someone we care about.

When I told Elizabeth what it was like to come home to that beautiful meal after the hard evening I had, I broke down in tears. She's been having a hard time too, she shared. I appreciated that, in the midst of her struggle, she wanted to share some love with my family. I gifted her with a bracelet of gratitude.

(And her tamales...Oh my word, they were amazing!!!)

Surprise food gifts=love.

Message of the day

Cook a meal or a treat for someone who might be going through a hard time
and surprise them!

Day 11

LAUGHTER IS THE BEST MEDICINE

One Saturday morning, I found myself driving across town in my husband's plus-size F150 in a distracted state, still processing some devastating news from the day before. The nifty new electronic gauge was telling me that I was down to three miles left in the tank. I asked Siri where the nearest gas station was and practically arrived on fumes at the pump. In Oregon, attendants are required to pump your gas, so I retrieved my credit card and waited while staring distractedly off into the distance.

I jumped when I heard a loud voice say, "What, are you trying to make me feel fat?"

I looked around to see the attendant shimmying past the side of the truck as he barely squeezed between the gas pump and my huge rig.

"Geez, I'm going to need to change my shirt after this," he said, wiping off the dusty dirt my car had left on his safety bib.

I laughed out loud. "Sorry, I forget how big this thing is."

"What will you have?" he asked.

After he started pumping, he came and stood by my window for a chat.

He said, "You seem nice, but we get some real weirdos in here. It's like Walmart on wheels. You wouldn't believe some of the interactions."

At this point Dean was on a roll and getting more and more animated telling me about his various interactions with people. My cheeks were beginning to hurt—I couldn't stop smiling.

"I think that everyone should be required to serve one year in the military and one year as a gas station attendant," he said. "Then everyone would be able to handle anything."

I was engaged now, out of my distracted state and feeling lighter. Dean ran over to start the pump on another car and then came back. "How old are you?" he asked me. I told him I was 42.

"Okay, let me ask you a question to someone of your generation. I've been thinking about this idea for a long time now—I just need some feedback. Do you use Facebook?"

"Um, yes, I do Dean," I said.

"Great. What do you think, what if I wore a GoPro while I pumped gas and posted daily funny interactions with people—like a reality gas station show? Do you think anyone would watch?"

I smiled. Yes, Dean—yes, I do.

Laughter really is the best medicine. Since I didn't have a bracelet that day, I decided to go back. I called the station and found out when Dean was working again. I brought a Christmas card, cash, and a bracelet. I pulled up to Dean's pump and told him, "I was having a really hard morning when I was here last Saturday, and your sense of humor changed the direction of my day and brought me joy during a really difficult time."

I handed him an envelope that had "Dean's GoPro Fund" written on the front. He laughed out loud and put his hand up for a high five. "So we are doing it then!" he said, and my hand slapping his was all the confirmation he needed.

Message of the day

Memorize a joke and look for a person who may need a good laugh today!

Day 12

COINCIDENCE?

I spent the day at Brendan's basketball game, cheering on the Bend Lava Bears. Before I left for the game, I put on two bracelets in Lava Bear colors, hoping I would encounter someone there who might be in need of a bracelet. The school came away with two wins, but I left without making any special connections.

Later that afternoon, I saw a man at the corner with a sign reading, "Anything helps." After asking him what he needed most, he replied, "Propane, because it's so darn cold right now." He lifted an empty propane tank from his bike trailer, and I loaded it in my car and left to find a place to fill it.

The first place I pulled into said their propane was frozen and not working.

So I drove farther down the road and found a gas station.

The woman in line in front of me smiled. Then she told me, "It's really nice what you are doing." Startled, as this gas station was a few miles from the corner where I picked up the tank, I asked her, "What do you mean?" She said, "I saw what you were doing back there, and it's a really nice thing. Most people have no idea what people are going through." I agreed. She paid for her things, smiled, and with a "God bless you, sweetie," she left. I was still amazed at the unlikelihood of our interaction.

The gas station attendant came and filled up my tank and I loaded it in my car. I drove back to the corner. It was getting dark. The man was packing up now, ready to head back to the woods while he still had some light.

He came over and we talked for a few minutes. He said his name was Charles, but everyone calls him Chappy. His dog, a beautiful German Shepherd name Mishka, did some tricks for me. He told me he grew up in Austin and was horribly addicted to drugs. At 42 years old, he had a life changing religious experience, and through faith and fellowship he has been sober now for 10 years. He worked for a local company framing houses but couldn't afford permanent housing.

When he looked up, I noticed his winter hat was blue with white writing. Upon further inspection, I noticed it said Bend High basketball. I unzipped my coat, showing him my Bend High basketball sweatshirt and told him what I had been doing all day. The hat, it turned out, was given to him by a boy that also lives in the woods—a boy who is homeless because his parents are both drug addicts. I took off the two bracelets and gave them to him. I told him that there are no coincidences, and that he was who I was supposed to meet today. I asked him to deliver the other bracelet to the boy and to let him know that there are people out there who do care about him.

Driving away, I passed Chappy and Mishka as they left. When I got home, I looked Chappy up on Facebook. I had told him about my Facebook Advent Challenge, and he mentioned that he used to have an account but hadn't been on in a while. His Facebook profile said it all. Chappy's job title was listed as Servant of God.

That's what it's all about! There are no coincidences.

Message of the day

When a coincidence arises, don't ignore it. Pay attention, look inward, and seek the message and significance of it. Trust that it was sent to you at the perfect time for the perfect reason.

Day 13

DON'T GRAB THE SCISSORS

Our youngest son, Jay Gordon Rosenzweig, was born on June 28, 2010. He was named Jay after the three main men in his life (Brian's middle name is Jay, my dad is Jim, and Brian's dad is Jeff). In memory of my grandfather, he has the middle name of Gordon. He just so happened to be born on my Dad's 65th birthday.

Eight months later, my dad was gone.

Jay's toddlerhood was a mixture of pure joy and pure grief for me. The highs were high and the lows were low. My Dad's unexpected death left me with a lot of internal things to examine, and pain and questioning to wade through. There were times I knew my Dad adored me, and times I wished he had shown up for me in ways he just didn't. I have immense love and appreciation for my dad, and in his absence, he had given me the gift of perspective and priorities.

What did I want my kids to know without a doubt?

What I do know is that Jay Gordon Rosenzweig loves his daddy. For Brian's birthday this year, I asked Jay what present he wanted to give his dad. He spent a few moments thinking, his hand on his chin and his eyes squinting. "Matching friendship bracelets," he declared, "because he's my best friend."

I happened to have some woven Kenyan bracelets that I knew would fit them both, so we wrapped them up and Jay presented the gift at his birthday dinner. "I got matching bracelets so we can be friendship buddies," Jay beamed.

Brian and Jay tied them on, proudly displaying their twin bracelets that signified their bond. As the weeks went by, I would hear them proclaim, "Friendship buddies!" Then they'd touch their wrists together and smile. They would help each other out, stick up for each other, go on movie outings together. And they became so proud of their bracelet bond that my other three kids got jealous!

Then there were the disagreements.

Whether it was the time Jay lost at a board game, didn't like his punishment, or felt disappointed with his dad, he would say in an angry or emotional state, "Give me the scissors, I'm cutting off my bracelet—you are not my friend anymore!" He would march around, all sad and frustrated, arms crossed, in distress. The rest of the family would gasp in horror—OH NO! Don't do it, don't cut off the friendship bracelet!

Always, the anger subsided, and Jay was relieved to still have his bracelet. The two would talk about the situation and how they reacted. It always ended with, "I'm sorry, I love you." He would say, "We are still best friends."

The bracelets have lasted seven months so far. They have been swimming in the ocean, the pool, the lake, and been worn through sick days and fun days. They are worn and frayed. Their vibrant colors have become washed out.

To me, their bracelets signify the bond we all have between kids and parents. Life will be messy and incredible and fun. It will also be painful and disappointing sometimes. But if you can weather the storms, the love that is so deep and rich and true always remains and sustains our bond: a bond that lasts forever, as long as we don't grab the scissors and cut ourselves off from it.

Message of the day

Think about your family today. Is there someone you want to recognize and appreciate for their connection with you? Or is there someone you might want to reach out to and repair or strengthen your connection?

Day 14

GET INSPIRED

Social media makes a lot of things look easy. A beautiful family posing happily, someone completing a marathon, a drool-worthy meal, a child receiving an award, the perfect selfie. The list goes on and on. It's easy to become disenchanted and disgruntled as I scroll Facebook and my kids are fighting, I don't feel like cooking, my kid just got a detention, and I can barely jog for 5 minutes. Often I end up getting annoyed, staring at all of the pretty people being so successful, and I feel like a failure—even though my life, with all its ups and downs, is truly amazing.

Maybe it's just me, but maybe you can relate.

I hate to exercise. (Which was fine, until I hit my 40s. Ouch.)

I'm not disciplined, so my occasional walk with a friend or yoga class here or there was not going to cut it. Every day I would see people on Facebook running marathons, doing crazy yoga poses, losing 50 pounds by eliminating sugar...You get my drift, right? I'm happy for all these people, but with each triumphant face I stared at, I felt overwhelmed. Where do I begin? That looks too hard. I could never do that.

Instead of inspired, I felt jealous.

How did they do that? How do they have the time?

Why are they smiling after running that long?

And before long I was bitter, disappointed, and still sitting on the couch.

Enter "Operation Get Inspired."

I have been going to Orange Theory Fitness now for 3 weeks—and it is hard. But I'm sticking with it. I'm getting stronger, and braver, and man I feel like a badass after each class.

And NOW, I can honestly say "thank you" to all of you Facebook people who post about your fitness achievements. I secretly hated you then, but I think you are total badasses now. Why? Because I joined you. I took the first, hard step: I stopped watching and started doing.

Brene Brown, in her book *Rising Strong,* says that there is a badassery deficit right now in our society. She said, "I know, badassery is a strange term, but I couldn't come up with another one that captures what I mean. When I see people stand fully in their truth, or when I see someone fall down, get back up, and say, 'Damn, that really hurt, but this is important to me and I'm going in again'—my gut reaction is, 'What a badass.'"

I gave my instructor an orange bracelet and told her that a great coach is super inspiring.

No longer will I be intimidated by the badasses. I am a badass.

At least for today.

Oh—and the picture sums up my love/hate relationship with exercise. I just finished burning 546 calories and I look like I want to punch her super happy face.

Message of the day

Whatever challenge you find most difficult in your life, find someone who is winning at it and who inspires you, and tell them! Then use them as a motivator to help you accomplish your goal!

Day 15

JUST ASK

If you saw a man on the corner holding this sign—what would you think?

What would you assume he needed?

What would you do?

Today, I rolled down the window and asked, "Which one of the things on your sign do you need most?"

He looked at the sign, then back at me and said "Honestly, probably food."

"Okay," I said, "What kind of food?"

Again he looked down, then back at me and admitted, "Honestly, I need meat the most."

That surprised me. "Meat?" I said, sounding confused. "What type of meat?"

"Oh, any old meat will do—hamburger, chicken, steak, anything you can eat, really."

"Like to grill?" I asked?

"Yes, we have a propane grill out at camp," he shared. "I cook for a whole group of people."

I told him I would go grab some meat and be right back. I drove a block to Safeway. As I walked back to the meat department, I realized that I was still surprised by his answer—I never would have guessed meat from looking at his sign. Honestly, I probably wouldn't have even rolled down my window, had I not been on this challenge to push myself out of my comfort zone and connect.

This is so true of everything in life, really. It's hard to look into the face of struggle. We never know what someone needs until we ask, even those closest to us. We avoid asking the uncomfortable questions and putting ourselves in vulnerable positions. We may make assumptions about what someone needs. We complicate things and sometimes even avoid them, instead of asking a really simple question: What do you need right now?

I returned to the corner and walked over with the bag of meat. I learned his name is Joe, and he was extremely appreciative. I gave him a bracelet and he thought it was awesome. I wished him well.

As I drove away, I promised to "just ask" the next time I noticed someone in a vulnerable position, whether it was my child in the middle of a meltdown or a person on the street corner—even if it made me uncomfortable or I don't know exactly what to say.

What do you need right now?

I may just be really surprised by the answer.

Message of the day

Ask someone today, "What do you need right now?"

Day 16

KEEP YOUR EYES OPEN

Today I went to Safeway to do my grocery shopping and hoped that I would see someone during my visit who I thought needed a bracelet. I walked each aisle, slowly and deliberately looking at each and every shopper, deli meat slicer, pharmacy tech, and cashier. As I approached each person, I would try to initiate eye contact and a smile. Only one or two shoppers even looked up. When I smiled at the few who did, they looked uncomfortable and hurried on their way.

As I was checking out, the bagger and cashier were having a conversation with each other, and I stood at the card reader pin pad observing their interaction. I saw an elderly gentleman walk in, with a Korean War vet hat on that rested softly on his hearing aids. He was pushing his cart with determination—and in that moment he reminded me of my grandfather, who I admired and missed terribly. The thought went through my mind that I wanted to wait for him to check out and pay for his groceries, thanking him for his service and wishing him a Merry Christmas.

I waited against the wall with my cart full of groceries, anxiously scanning the checkout lines for him to appear. I pushed my cart back and forth, hoping I would catch a glimpse of him so that I could prepare the cashier for my plan.

I waited, and waited, and waited. After about 30 minutes of waiting (no joke), I realized I somehow must have missed him. Maybe he came for one item and left.

As I made my way outside in the darkness at 25 degrees, I looked over and saw a woman sitting alone on a bench. She seemed out of place to me, so I made a point to make eye contact with her. I smiled a big smile and said hello. She smiled back and as I pushed my cart next to her, she said, "May I ask you a question?"

"Of course!" I said.

"Can you help me with something?" she asked me.

"I would love to."

"I need something. I need help. I need…" She hesitated.

"I need some feminine products," she blurted.

My eyes got big, as this was not at all what I was expecting. "Of course!" I told her. After asking her details about what she needed, I went in and made my purchase.

When I returned to the cold darkness, she thanked me with a big hug and told me I had no idea how much she appreciated this. She told me her name was Ashley, and that she had been out of work since Thanksgiving. She had fallen and broken her arm, lost her job, and spent all of her money on medical bills.

I gave her a bracelet and explained the meaning behind it. She put it on and told me all about her Uncle Carl who lived in Uganda with the Peace Corps. "I can't wait to tell Uncle Carl all about this."

As I left, I told Ashley that I felt we were meant to meet that day. She said, "I was just waiting for the right person to come out—and as soon as you looked at me, I knew that was you."

As I pushed my cart to my car, I saw the Korean War vet pushing his cart across the parking lot. Inside his cart were three 12-packs of Coca-Cola, and that made me smile.

Message of the day

Spend time today making eye contact and smiling at everyone you encounter. See who may smile back—and tell them "thank you!"

Day 17

COMPASSION

2017 was the worst year of my life. Okay, I take that back...not the worst, THE HARDEST. And for me—and maybe you can relate—hardest equals worst.

I prefer easy, happy, and conflict-free.

Words to describe the year: messy, painful, terrifying, gut-wrenching, sad, hopeless, and emotionally draining. We suffered immensely; I'm not going to sugar coat it. Our small circle was dealt some serious health issues, both physical and mental, and they were grave.

But here is what I have learned:

Pain is where wisdom and strength are born (Brene Brown).

There is no greater gift you can give someone than to walk next to them through the struggle, each and every hard step. To show up when it's messy, and stay. And love. And stand tall and not shrink. And tell them that you don't know what comes next, but that you love them no matter what.

I've learned that courage is contagious.

I've learned that no one can help you if you don't ask.

And I have learned the true meaning of COMPASSION.

A friend reminded me that the word "compassion" comes from the Latin root "passio" which means to suffer, paired with the Latin prefix "com" which means together. So compassion literally means to suffer TOGETHER. It requires community. And as Christian theologian Thomas Aquinas states, "no one becomes compassionate unless he suffers."

We aren't meant to suffer alone. Yet we also don't always know how to ask for help. Buddhist teachings instruct that compassion is when "the heart trembles in the face of suffering," that your heart opens instead of closes.

So with that being said, one day I came across a simple statement by a stranger on Facebook that made my own heart tremble, and made me curious. Sometimes being curious is the first step to compassion. This woman, Carol, mentioned that she just moved out of rehab and into a sober living house. Then she said, "Many of the women have no one, and it would be nice for them to feel loved." I reached out to Carol and asked what the home she lived in might need.

After a few replies back and forth, Carol stated that what they really needed was silverware, scented candles, and body lotions. "The women like things that calm them and comfort them." That was all I needed to hear, and I understood exactly what Carol and the women needed.

They needed comfort during the struggle. They needed to feel loved when times were grave. They needed everything I had learned and experienced this year. I was in.

I ran to Target and TJ Maxx, grabbing nail polish and body spray, silverware and scented candles. I brought them to the sober living house and was invited in to chat with Carol (newly sober), Tina (45 days in) and Sally (90 days the following day!). They were open, honest, and vulnerable. They said that they wouldn't be sober if it weren't for each other. They said that living in this house was the first time they had felt safe. Tina said she watches the clock at work, waiting for the minute she can come home to the group. These women struggle every day, together. They attend 3 to 5 meetings a day. They hope to reconnect with their families. They are gaining strength and wisdom through their pain. Their courage is contagious.

They each picked out a bracelet, and it was so wonderful to watch. I got warm hugs from each—and honestly, I could have talked all night. I told them that whenever they wore their bracelet, I hope they remembered that we are connected, and that I care about them and am inspired by them. They said that, with addiction, "Sometimes we feel like no one cares, and this shows us that is not true—especially during the holidays when we are prone to relapse." They said, "thank you," and I later got a message from Carol that said I was their angel.

The gift of suffering together is priceless. Love and strength to these brave women—and so much love to everyone who showed us compassion knowingly or unknowingly in our hard times. You are our angels.

Message of the day

How can you show compassion to someone struggling today?

Day 18

VULNERABILITY

This Power of Connection Challenge is just that: a challenge. Each and every day I am challenged to complete the task of connecting with someone in a vulnerable way. It could be called the Vulnerability Challenge.

Not only is this the busy holiday season, but add in family commitments, self-care, and work, and it's easy to see why taking the time to connect with people in real and vulnerable ways is a rarity in our world these days. It's HARD!

I know firsthand that it can be hard to ask for help. We think we can handle things ourselves, don't want to burden those we care about, and all the other stories we tell that keep us closed up, alone with our thoughts and feelings.

Brene Brown says, "Staying vulnerable is a risk we have to take if we want to experience connection."

When I saw a post today about a mom who needed diapers for her son because she had no money and was using the last of her paycheck to pay for gas to get her son to a doctor's appointment, I immediately reached out. She told me the size and that she needed wipes too, if I wouldn't mind.

What did I do when she had the courage to ask for help?

I responded. I reached out. I connected with her.

We decided to meet at Walmart before her son's appointment. For some reason, a post about Walmart having diapers on sale had been across my Facebook feed three or four times in the previous few days (—there are no coincidences!), so I knew where to find the best deal.

I purchased them and headed out to meet her for the delivery. I had given her a description of where I parked, and as I approached my car, I saw her sitting in the passenger seat of her vehicle. She gave a little wave, then quickly got out and came over. Looking slightly uncomfortable with the generosity of a stranger, she reached out her arms to accept the diapers and wipes. "Thank you so much," she said. "I have no money left. This means the world to me."

When she looked up and our eyes locked, I said, "Every day this month I am trying to do something nice for someone, and today that person is you. Thank you for letting me help you."

She replied with a beautiful smile. "Well then, I am so glad I put my request out there today and that I got to be your person."

"Me, too," I replied.

That is what being vulnerable looks like, friends. The courage to ask and the courage to answer.

I explained to her that the women in Kenya have asked for help, too. They are desperate to help their girls thrive by continuing their education and providing skills training. She can wear her bracelet to remind her that powerful shifts happen by being vulnerable and asking for what we need.

Message of the day

Be on the lookout to help someone who shows vulnerability and asks for what they need.

Day 19

HOME

I have lived in Bend, Oregon, for 17 years. Bend is a great place to live and it's the only home my kids have ever known. It's a small mountain town in central Oregon, home to about 90,000 people.

However, my home was Georgia. I lived there 28 years. I grew up in an amazing family neighborhood (shout out to the Creekers), I met my husband in high school there (go, Greyhounds!), I went to college there (go, Dawgs!), and I developed the deep roots of who I am there, thanks to the amazing people who supported and loved me along the way.

Moving cross-country and starting brand-new in the Pacific Northwest at the age of 28 was terrifying and exhilarating. We swapped sweet tea and Chick-Fil-A for farm-to-table, kombucha, and microbrews. We stopped the "y'alls" and "bless your heart's, and our kids' teachers asked them not to call them ma'am or sir. We have adapted and grown. We own skis, mountain bikes, paddleboards, and Patagonia. It's fourteen years later, and we have established our own deep roots here in the high desert.

But sometimes I just miss my home.

So no one would prepare me for the facts I am about to tell you.

In my neighborhood,

in my small mountain town,

there is not one,

not two,

not three,

but FOUR families with ties to the UNIVERSITY OF GEORGIA, y'all!

I delivered two UGA-colored Kenyan friendship bracelets one day to two ladies who I have leaned on these past few weeks in hard times. Mimi and Deedee are UGA alums and they both LIVE IN MY NEIGHBORHOOD! Whaaaat?

So I dropped off bracelets to them and Mimi said, "I am not deserving of these bracelets—why do I get one?" And I simply answered, "Because you are home to me." She knew exactly what I meant.

After I left Mimi and Deedee (I can hear all of you Southerners pronounce those names as I type them!), I drove back to my neighborhood. Because guess what? Mimi told me she saw a house with a Georgia flag on her street.

Well, that was all I needed. I spotted the flag a mile away, and I pulled into the driveway and marched up to the door. There was a sign by the door declaring this UGA fan's loyalty. I knocked and waited with sheer excitement. A woman and her daughter answered, and I told them that I was a crazy southerner who went to Georgia and had to say hello! Turned out her husband was the Georgia fan, and they had just moved here three months ago, and our daughters actually attended school together. I gave her a bracelet and my number and promised a get-together soon.

As I was leaving, I saw her husband waiting to pull in. I did not hesitate—I jogged up to the window and he rolled it down. Look at his picture I'm sharing to see why this interaction was truly gold. We high-fived, laughed, and swapped Georgia stories. We are literally new best friends already, because that's how I was raised to do it in the south.

(You can take a girl out of Georgia, but you can't take Georgia out of the girl.)

Message of the day

Take a moment to appreciate someone in your life who feels like home to you.

Day 20

JUST DO IT

It's really very simple, so don't overthink this:

DO SOMETHING POSITIVE.

DO SOMETHING WITH LOVE.

DO SOMETHING THAT HELPS SOMEONE ELSE.

It doesn't have to be a big something or something done perfectly. It's easy to make excuses like, "I will do something, just not right now," or "I don't know what to do," or "Whatever I do won't matter." Start with small things, rooted in love and connection. Mother Teresa said, "In this life we cannot always do great things. But we can do small things with great love."

My dear friend wanted to buy a large quantity of bracelets, but she didn't quite know who to give them to. I remembered that there was a therapeutic boarding school for girls in my hometown. I sent an email, asking if we could gift the girls a bracelet. I received a return email with an enthusiastic YES—23 girls would be thrilled to receive a bracelet. The plan was to do a short presentation on Kenya, tell the girls about women's education in Kenya, and then pass out bracelets.

When I arrived, I met 23 girls, ages 10 to 15. They came from all over the country: New York, LA, San Francisco, Connecticut, to name a few. They were very curious about the bracelets and specifically why anyone would want to buy them for people they didn't know.

You might have your own opinions and feelings about therapeutic boarding schools. However, haven't we all hit a "failure to thrive" period? To me it's no different than the women at the sober living house having hit rock bottom, or the homeless who live meal-to-meal, friends struggling through a marriage that is ending, someone battling mental illness or career unhappiness, or watching your child struggle and feeling powerless, suffering a devastating illness, or maybe just going through a phase when you forget who you are or who you are meant to be.

Failure to thrive happens.

So when I look at these teens and pre-teens who are far away from home and trying to find their way, I have so much love for them. Their hard work in the face of adversity inspires me. I tell them that this bracelet connects us. It connects them to the woman who generously bought all 23 bracelets because she cares about you. It connects them to the women in Kenya, who are beautiful and struggling, too. It connects them to each other—

may they always support and love each other. It connects them to this moment in their life—may they always remember their struggle and the wisdom and strength that comes from it.

After my presentation, the girls each chose a bracelet. They stared at them and turned them over in their hands. They were emotional as they looked at the pictures of the Kenyan women. Then their instructor asked, "Do any of you want to use your own account money to purchase additional bracelets?" Every hand went up. These girls are sending girls in Kenya to school. In the midst of their own struggle, they want to help other girls, and they're making a choice to do something to change it.

Message of the day

I encourage you, that in dark and negative times, or whenever you feel lonely, fearful or lost, DO SOMETHING. Something positive. Something with love. Something that helps someone else.

Day 21

AREN'T WE ALL FRIENDS?

Today Jay (6) was stir-crazy since our cold, snowy weather has kept us housebound more than usual. After he "accidentally" knocked his sister off the couch during an indoor wrestling match, he and I decided to set out to find a new friend together. We came across a woman bundled up in the cold with a sign that said, "Anything is appreciated, even kindness."

I asked Jay if he would like to come meet the woman on the corner. "YES!" he shouted.

We got out and asked the woman, whose name was Vickie, what she needed most right now. "A warm sleeping bag," she shared. She hadn't been able to get to her camp in the woods due to all the recent snow.

Jay and I told her we would run to Dick's (our new favorite place) and grab her a sleeping bag.

Jay was so excited. We looked through all of the available bags on the shelves, and Jay pointed out the one he wanted to get Vickie. "It's blue, like her eyes," he said. I had noticed her gorgeous blue eyes, too, almost aquamarine in color.

We got to the counter to check out, and Jay announced, "We are buying this for a lady." The clerk asked if we were buying it for the Bethlehem Inn. "No," Jay told the clerk, "It's for the lady out on the corner—she needs a bed," he said. "She doesn't have a house, and she's cold," Jay uttered matter-of-factly.

Jay skipped out of the store. He was so excited to deliver the goods. We walked over to Vickie and handed her the bag. She was so grateful. She had a huge smile and a hearty laugh. I asked her if I detected a Southern accent, and she corrected me that she was born and raised in the Midwest. She asked Jay if he had been good this year and if Santa was coming to see him soon. "I hope so," he responded, "because sometimes I act a little bad." Vickie laughed. "Don't we all!" Jay told her that she had pretty eyes, and she laughed out loud. "I hear that from all the men."

I gave her a bracelet and she thanked us for caring. As we walked back to our car, Jay asked why I didn't ask Vickie for her phone number. "Why?" I asked. "Because you two are friends now," he said. Yes, Jay, we are. We drove past Vickie and her sign and Jay waved excitedly. "Bye Vickie!" he yelled out the window—and just like that, he has been happier all day.

Message of the day

Go out of your way to make a new friend today!

Day 22

CAREGIVERS

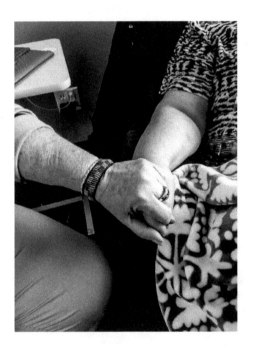

I had to stop by the hospital one day for an appointment, and afterward I passed by the infusion center. I walked in and asked the nurses if there was anyone who could use a little love and company. They looked at each other and unanimously pronounced, "Evelyn." They checked with Evelyn to see if she was up for a random, unannounced visitor. Apparently, she was! I was led back to her room and sat down to make small talk.

Evelyn said it had been a really hard year. Evelyn was diagnosed with cancer in June and has visited this center twelve hours a week, every other week, since then.

This week she had a port placed, "Because the veins in my arms had given up," she said, showing me her bruised arms. "It's very sore," she lamented, and gently placed her hand over her port as she started to tear up. I asked her if she had family support. She lit up and exclaimed, "Yes! My husband Tom is my best friend in the whole world, and he is the only reason I am able to get through this. He stays with me, he takes care of me, and he is my everything." (Tom was out getting her lunch in the snowy whiteout conditions). "The man upstairs will take care of us," she told me. "It's going to be Okay."

I told Evelyn about my bracelet and asked her if I could give her one, too. She accepted it and rolled it around in her hand for a moment. "I would actually like to give it to Belinda," she shared. "Belinda is my nurse and she—well, all the ladies here for that matter—they are my angels. They take such good care of me."

Through her darkest time, Evelyn feels taken care of. She wanted to offer the same feeling back to those who care for her.

We called Belinda back in the room and told her of our exchange. We told her of her angel appreciation. Evelyn chose a bracelet for Belinda and she put it on. I was able to witness the love and appreciation they both had for each other. They held hands and squeezed hard, as if to say, "We are in this together." Belinda then told me that she was about to leave to take chemo infusions to homebound patients who couldn't drive in the winter storm. She said she drives a Volkswagen Beetle, so driving could be interesting in our winter conditions. Somehow, I hope her bracelet will remind her of her angel appreciation from so many patients she has already touched, and from those she will love and care for in the future.

This is for all of the caregivers, nurses, doctors AND patients: may you have a deep sense of being taken care of, loved, and appreciated. Keep fighting!

Message of the day

Caregivers nourish, support, love, encourage, and heal those around us every day. Reach out to a caregiver you know, and thank them for the very important job they do.

Day 23

BE A DO-ER

I realized that, during this month-long challenge, all of my kids had experienced the gift of helping others, except for my oldest child, Brendan. He is in high school and tends to either be playing basketball, doing homework, playing video games, or something that involves being in the confines of his room. We don't get to see enough of his smiling face, so today I took him with me to find a person to help.

We pulled up to a small man on the corner, hunched over his walker. We rolled down the window and asked him what he needed most. "Long underwear, actually," he said. "I am a small pant and a medium top." We told our new friend we would grab him these items and be right back.

As soon as I rolled the window back up, Brendan told me, "Mom, I can't believe I didn't go with you every day this month. This is so amazing. He was so nice."

We ran into Costco and bought two sets of long underwear. As we walked back to the car, Brendan was asking lots of questions about what the homeless may or may not need.

We walked back up the hill and stood and talked to our new friend. He was extremely appreciative of his gifts. He stays warm in his tent, he explained, due to five sleeping bags that he sleeps under. Tom then said with a laugh, "But at some point, you have to get up and get moving, and that's when I get cold."

I gave Tom a bracelet and explained its meaning, and he said he was really happy to wear it. We chatted a bit longer and wished Tom a Merry Christmas.

As we walked away, Brendan had some realizations. He told me he felt selfish and that he wasn't readily looking for ways to help others. He explained that a lot of people want to help, but not many actually do it. "I want to be a do-er," he stated—and I think he will.

Message of the day

Kids need role models who will help them to see service in action.
How can you find a way to take someone along and do an act of service
today so that we can encourage a generation of do-ers?

Day 24

BE A FAN

Last week at my oldest son's basketball game, a cheery-faced young man walked over during warm-ups. He had a huge grin and said to me, "I'm Jonny. I love Bend High basketball."

I introduced myself, and he stood there beaming. I couldn't help but catch his contagious happy spirit. As the team came back to the bench, I watched Jonny high five each and every player and the coach.

As I sat in the stands, I watched Jonny walk around the gym, smiling and greeting people. He cheered the team at every play and jumped up and down with the victory.

When I got home, I told Brendan about meeting Jonny and asked if Brendan knew of him since he seemed to interact with all of the players.

Brendan pulled out a hand-written letter that he had received before the game. It was from Jonny. It read, "Hey Brendan Rosenzweig you are doing a great job playing forward for the Lava Bears Basketball Team. You are my favorite forward at Bend High Lava Bears Basketball Brendan. From your Bend High Fan, Class of '04, Jonny Goddard."

Apparently, Jonny wrote a personal letter to every member of the team.

I knew I had to give this super fan a bracelet. His kindness and encouragement needed to be recognized, as well as his contagious spirit.

The next night, when I arrived at the game, Jonny was walking around with his usual smile. As I approached him, not knowing if he remembered me, he stood up, smiled, and immediately put his arms out for a huge hug. I told him I had a special Lava Bear bracelet for him, and he quickly put it on. He told me all about his love for basketball, and that his favorite team of all time is, of course, always Bend High's team.

I stood next to him for a quarter, watching his enthusiasm and excitement for every play, and told him I wanted a picture with he and Brendan after the game. He happily agreed.

After the game, he came and stood next to me, waiting for the players to emerge from their post-game talk in the locker room. As they did, I called Brendan over to take the picture of him and Jonny. Then, one by one, Jonny had his picture taken with each of the members of the team. He was grinning from ear to ear.

A true fan is someone who stands by their team in good times and bad and is enthusiastically devoted. This can apply to a person in your life as well as your favorite sports team.

Standing by someone through good and bad times and being enthusiastically devoted is a gift. Thank you for blessing us with your enthusiasm, Jonny Goddard!

Message of the day

Tell someone today why you are their biggest fan!

Day 25

GOALS

Christmas was just around the corner and I was not ready! I still had a long list of to-do's and, the night before, I could feel the beginnings of a cold brewing. I'd started this challenge to slow down and look for the meaning of the season and for the connections all around us. However, "life" had gotten busy, noisy and stressed.

Thankfully, I had a Christmas angel remind me of what is important that very day!

I was dropping off 5 bracelets to my friend at her restaurant in town. She and I were digging through all the styles and choices so she could find the perfect ones for her family. As she left to grab her money, I took that moment to ponder my next stop in my long list of errands. I happened to look over and see a woman sitting at the end of the bar, relaxed and peaceful, deep into a book, and sipping a margarita every few pages.

I walked over to her and said "I have to come meet you. You are the exact opposite of how I am feeling right now. I have to know your secret, because I feel rushed, run down and crazy this time of year."

She smiled, lifted her margarita and said, "This is called retirement."

I almost fell over and died.

We went on to chat for half an hour. Her name was Chris. She lived a few blocks down the street and came here for lunch "most days of the week."

We talked about our kids, vacations, careers, marriage, and the crazy roller coaster of life.

She visits the library and checks out and finishes three books every week. She likes to hike. She sent money to her kids and grandkids, no shopping required. Her Christmas plans were equally simple and perfect, prime rib at a friend's house.

Her life motto: "Moderation."

This was just the message I needed to hear today.

In the midst of the chaos, the lists and the rushing...here was someone who was choosing balance, peace and connection.

I told her to pick out a bracelet, (which my friend Carol paid for as a gift to Chris), and asked her for a photo.

"I need a picture of my future life goals," I told her, "and next time I am joining you for lunch."

"Come any day dear..." Chris said.

As I left, I heard a waitress ask her how her day was going and she replied, "I just got this beautiful bracelet..."

Slow down, simplify, enjoy, connect...moderation.

Message of the day

How can you find "moderation" in the midst of today?

Day 26

RESPECT

My son Brendan has "mad respect" for his Pre-Calculus teacher Ross Torkelson.

As this school year has progressed they have formed quite a unique bond.

"Tork," as the kids call him, has been teaching math for over three decades.

One day, in the first few weeks of this school year, Brendan was hungry during math class and proceeded to take out some leftover pizza from his backpack and eat while Tork was teaching. Tork has a no eating policy in class. He also has a great sense of humor. So, he asked Brendan if he was thirsty and would like a refreshing beverage to go with his pizza. Brendan, confused at this question, said "I guess...that...would...be nice?"

Then Tork proceeded to go over to his mini fridge and get out a cold, refreshing RC cola and hand it to Brendan for him to enjoy. He also took a paper towel and neatly placed it in the collar of Brendan's shirt for full effect.

Then he went about teaching. The class was totally dumbfounded.

Every week since then, in a random and unexpected moment, Tork will pause class and offer Brendan a cold RC cola while the rest of the class looks around in bewilderment.

There have been other funny moments. Once Tork had the foods teacher interrupt class to bring in a meal for Brendan complete on a silver platter. Delivered by a waiter in a tux, who proceeded to put down a white tablecloth on Brendan's desk. The class roared in laughter.

Then there was the time Brendan came to school dressed just like Tork, with a nametag that said "Mr. Borkelson," and proceeded to teach the class while Tork sat in a student desk and drank RC cola.

Or the time the students made Tork stickers with their favorite Tork quotes.

"Tork is a true master in the art of teaching."

"He balances teaching the skills and knowledge of the subject along with care, humor, humanity and connection."

Something kids today need more and more of...adults in their corner.

When I asked Brendan if he wanted to give Tork a bracelet, he said yes. He picked one out in blue and gold, the school colors. Brendan told me that Tork was such a great teacher because he "invests in all of his students, connects with them and shows us what hard work looks like. He has missed so few days in his teaching career, that if he used all of his days he has saved up, he could take a year off! He is funny, understanding and amazing at teaching math. He also pushes us to be better because he cares about each of us. Oh, and he is a legend."

So today, Brendan convinced his entire math class to dress up like their teacher (sweaters and all) to pay homage to their beloved Tork. It was epic. Tork told Brendan, "It is so nice to be appreciated. Lately it seems that all I hear is the negative. So this means the world to me."

I included a picture of the class, all making the classic Tork pose, which he uses when he is emphasizing something important.

I hope today, he felt just how important he is to these kids.

"Mad respect" for you, Tork—from very appreciative Brendan's mom.

Message of the day

Who deserves some respect today?

Day 27

DREAMS

A post from a Heather came across my Bend Pay it Forward feed:

"What's the fastest way to raise money to get a plane ticket?!? I just got the call that my grandma isn't going to make it much longer. I am trying to get home (GA) to say my good-byes!!"

My heart sank...I knew all too well about having to get that news. My mom and I rushed to Austin in the same way, to be with my grandmother when we got the call.

I sent Heather a message and offered to help.

The Pay it Forward fundraiser had raised some money so far, so I decided to see what kind of ticket I could find for her. We discussed dates, cheaper airports and different airlines. However, long story short...holiday travel is outrageously expensive! After we had tried everything, Heather and I decided that it was not meant to be.

Heather wrote, "I'm very thankful for you trying. I'm praying my check on the 24th is enough to even do Christmas. I doubt I will make it to Georgia anytime soon."

I replied, "I will keep looking for you. I saw that last month you asked for help to go to back to school. I would like to know the best way to help out. I do have some funds, just want to help in the best way I can."

She got really excited. "Honestly the best way to help out is getting COCC paid off so that I could go to school. I had given up on going to school because I still owe $636 from when I went and got my CNA. I have no way to pay it. I already applied to start the prerequisites for nursing on January 7. I have applied for grants, scholarships and financial aid as well. They won't let me do anything until I pay off what I owe."

After we chatted some more, I learned that she is a 28-year-old Georgia girl (from Macon) and has a 7-year-old son, TJ, who is severely autistic. She works full time as a CNA and has always dreamed of being an RN and an ASL interpreter. I couldn't help but get drawn to this Southern mama, who was trying hard to get by, called me ma'am, and had given up on her dreams.

I agreed to meet her the next day at the Admissions office to help pay off her balance. She was so excited. "I have been looking up school stuff all day, lol, I'm such a school nerd, school makes me happy."

When we met up at the college, she told me to "look for the girl with the bow in her hair"...GOD BLESS her and her hair bow! (All of you Georgians should smile at that).

She was beaming. She couldn't wait to inform me that the financial aid office agreed to apply $200 to her balance. They also approved her for next term.

That left her balance due at $436.

The Pay it Forward fundraiser had raised $437.

Just like that...we are sending another girl to school.

She registered for classes on the spot.

As I stood there chatting with her about life, her future and her family, she proudly exclaimed that this was the BEST thing that has ever happened to her. That she had NO WORDS for what this meant. That she was excited to fulfill her DREAMS. As she pushed open the door to head outside, I couldn't help but think how her future changed in this one moment.

Thanks to a whole lot of Earth angels, changing the world one bracelet and one dollar at a time. Together we can make a difference!

Message of the day

Who needs some hope that their dreams come true today?

Day 28

SAIGE

A local mom wanted to get her daughter an American Girl doll for Christmas but she was not able to afford one. She posted a plea on Facebook, looking to see if anyone had one they wanted to pass on. This was the only thing her daughter wanted for Christmas and she really wanted to help make her Christmas wish come true. She just needed some help.

I knew Rachel had some dolls in storage. She had quietly packed them away once she entered middle school. A subtle sign that she was leaving her childhood and innocence behind. I knew that she had more than enough to share with this little girl.

She was home from school when I informed her of the little girl and the Christmas wish. She was freshly reeling from negative school drama and this change of focus made her eyes light up.

Still, I could tell she was struggling with the idea of letting this symbolic part of her childhood go. I gave her the choice and told her there was no pressure.

A few moments later she came to me with a plan and she asked me to bring the tote out of storage. As the day progressed, "Saige" was lovingly chosen. Rachel held her, dressed her up, and washed and styled her hair.

She chose some accessories to send with her and I watched as she carefully packed a bag. She tenderly prepared the doll for her new owner and I softened as I watched my baby girl stand with one foot in her childhood and one right on the edge of teenage-world.

We loaded up to deliver "Saige" and drove to Elizabeth's work. We pulled up and parked. I looked over and Rachel was cradling her baby one more time...I swear she was mentally saying her goodbyes. Elizabeth came out to greet us and literally jumped for joy at the doll.

"Oh my gosh, she's perfect. My daughter is literally going to scream when she opens her on Christmas." She embraced Rachel in a big hug.

I then gave her a bracelet and explained that each day I was finding someone to help, and that this day it was her. She started to cry and took a moment to compose herself. "I was at a point where I didn't think there was good in the world anymore. My sister was taken from me, and murdered by her boyfriend. All I could see was evil. This bracelet and this doll are almost too much. It tells me that there is good in the world. I have to remember there is so much good."

We told her of Rachel's experience of an outpouring of love last night in a really difficult time. We told her that we now knew that love trumped hate. She replied, "I will wear this and remember! I will also send you a picture of my daughter opening this gift on Christmas morning!"

As we drove away, we both knew that "Saige" would be loved.

Message of the day

Let your child choose a special toy they have outgrown and gift it to a child in need. They will have a unique and forever connection.

Day 29

LOVE TRUMPS HATE

Hey girl, thought I'd let you know that you're amazing. Do not let anybody or anyone tell you different. Life gets hard and we all have our struggles but I promise it all happens for a reason. You're a beautiful soul in and out and you can change the world someday with your kindness. Hope you have a great day tomorrow and remember to smile don't let others get you down 🖤

Without going into details, my daughter Rachel had now officially experienced what it feels like to be bullied, both in person and by text. It created feelings of sadness, rejection and frankly, fear. She stayed home from school yesterday as multiple nasty texts poured in and we pondered what our next best step was.

Bullying is everywhere and no one is exempt from the possibility that it might happen to them. There are campaigns and public service announcements trying to educate and curb its abuse and frequency. However, it has and always will exist because there will always be some hate in the world.

The whole family spent the day wrestling with the situation. We vacillated between anger and sadness. We were in disbelief, yet trying to make sense of it all. However, all the focus was on the negative, the hate. How to avoid it, how to ignore it, and how to stop it.

Then my oldest son Brendan, in his infinite wisdom of 16 years of age, made a split-second decision that was nothing short of a miracle. He chose love.

Unbeknownst to us, he sent a snapchat out to his contacts that told of Rachel's situation at school. Then he added the following message: "My sister doesn't even want to go to school anymore, it's really hard on her and nobody should be treated like this. Will everyone please take a moment out of their day to text her and just tell her she's beautiful and kind, or just send a nice message? It would mean so much to me, and her. Thank you."

Rachel and I were driving Jay to soccer and her phone received a text. "Mom, why is Morgan sending me a text? Did Brendan tell her what is happening?" She looked at me anxiously. Then another. And another. All night long, texts from friends and strangers alike...filling her phone with words of encouragement, stories of their own bullying and how they got through it, and inspiring words of hope. It was incredible.

Words telling her she was beautiful, she mattered, she was not alone, she was loved, she was supported, she was strong, and advice on how to move forward. She received over 300 positive messages.

I had spoken of Earth angels, people who comfort, guide and protect us...well here it was in action. Rachel was surrounded by Earth angels and it was a powerful force that shifted the entire situation. Yes, she still had a wound, but the Band-Aid of love provided by others quickly sped up the healing process. This strong sense of connection was all it took to stomp out the negativity. She was literally skipping around our house that night.

The real hero award goes to brother Brendan, who shared her struggle and asked for help—who chose light and love over revenge, anger or isolation.

When we ask for help, people will show up. They are WAITING to show up. Teenage boys and girls sent looooong texts to a young girl they didn't even know because they CARED. This is humanity at its finest.

There are kids hurting every day from bullying who don't have a tribe of Earth angels, who don't have a supportive family, who don't have a place to turn, and who don't ask for help. We had lost one of those dear kids last year in our community, and we couldn't help but think the night before at our dinner table how something like this could have helped him feel supported, loved, and protected.

Community is collective, and if we want our community to thrive, we have to choose to focus on the good, to spread love, to be love.

Teenagers are accused all the time of being too self-focused and selfie/image driven. Well, this day changed my perspective forever. Teens are waiting to have a platform to help, to love and to care. Someone just has to be vulnerable enough to ask.

We have to keep working to make it okay to say, "I am struggling. I need help."

When we do that, we open the door for the calvary of support and love to rush in...and that helps love win.

I was the new champion of all high schoolers...everywhere. To teens, I want to say: you all have the power and the hearts to change the world!!!!! One snapchat at a time.

I have included pictures of just some of the texts she received...thank you to everyone who pitched in to help.

I took all the texts and copied them and I will turn them into a book Rachel can reflect back on. I will title it-

"Love trumps hate. Sincerely, your Earth angels."

Message of the day

Spread some love on social media today.

Day 30

GRATITUDE

We had been without heat and hot water since the previous Thursday. That was 6 days. In frigid temperatures. We had our fireplaces constantly burning and had burned through half a cord of wood already. We had slept in coats and hats, piled into beds together to keep warm. We had taken minimal amounts of showers at our local athletic club, washed hair in sinks, and were smelling/looking pretty rough!

It's amazing what happens when you have to go without your daily comforts and conveniences. You get irritated. You whine and complain. But then you slowly realize just how lucky you had it!

On day 7, my hero rode in with his yellow van and saved the day. He had come each of the 6 days (even Saturday and Sunday), trying different parts and solutions. Before he got to work, he looked at me and said, "If you and the family need to come to my house and take showers, our door is open!"

In a scene just like out of the Christmas story, where the dad is hammering away at the boiler, Bob restored the machine and life got a little warmer.

This made me reflect on how much we take for granted. Sure, we were inconvenienced for a time, but our life would return to normal. I talked to people every day who live without a roof over the head or a shower to clean in.

As Bob packed up to leave, I told him about my Power of Connection project. I said that today, he was deserving of my bracelet. Our family was definitely grateful for the service, perseverance and hard work he provided to bring back our heat.

He picked out a colorful one that reminded him most of Africa, he said.

The women in Kenya were trying to send their girls to school. They didn't have the luxury of equal education for women, so they were working hard to make these bracelets, in hopes that each person's purchase would afford them this chance. I guarantee they didn't take even $1 for granted.

Then I spent time in gratitude in the shower!

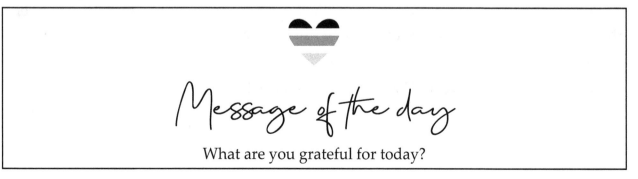

Message of the day

What are you grateful for today?

Day 31

ANGELS

Perfect! And do you need twin bedding?

Thankyou again I cant tell you how much I appreciate it

Happy to help out a fellow mama!

You are an angel truly

I noticed a post on Facebook—a mom looking for a twin bed for her 4-year-old toddler. She was new to town and the air mattress he had been sleeping on popped, leaving him sleeping on the floor.

Knowing that the Power of Connection Advent Challenge fundraiser had been gifted money, I reached out to let her know that I would love to pick up a twin bed and deliver it to her. She was thrilled.

"You are an angel, truly," she responded.

Soon after we messaged, a bike came across the same feed. A woman was paying forward a bike that her son had outgrown. I messaged that I would love to pick it up as well and deliver to this mama and her kiddo, a perfect gift for Christmas!

As I drove to pick up the mattress, I thought about how it felt to be called an angel. Angels, to me, are divine spirits who we can call on to help guide, protect and comfort us.

I, on the other hand, am only human, imperfectly human I might add, trying to do my best to help others. Calling me an angel was a stretch that felt too overwhelming and undeserving.

As I pondered this idea, it occurred to me that what is missing in the world today is the ability to look for the divine meaning in everything and everyone.

A gift or service that you can provide that someone else needs.

An interaction that brings comfort or healing.

A nudge that tells you to help someone.

A message that comes at the right time.

A miracle.

We are all spiritual beings, living a human life, and we can all look for ways to guide, protect and comfort each other—to be each other's Earth angels.

With the mattress and bike in tow...I arrived at Leeya's house. She came out to greet me and had a serene, kind presence. She embraced me in a long hug, and softly said, "Thank you so much. You are my angel." I smiled, accepting the words in this moment. "I am honored to help," I said. We took the mattress inside and hid the bike, so that she could surprise her son for Christmas. I visited a bit, met her son, and gifted them both bracelets.

As I left, Leeya gave me another big hug. As I drove home, I smiled to myself over our connection. She messaged me soon after. She was moved by the Power of Connection project and wanted to help. She told me that her partner was an electrician, and that they both wanted to help me pay it forward this month, if the opportunity presented itself.

There it was. Connection makes the world a more divine space. When we act from our heart, from our soul, we create a ripple effect of divine love that this world so desperately needs. I felt grateful to the angels who donated to the fundraiser so far, making this possible. I sent thanks to the angel who donated the bike. I thanked the angels who guided me to read the initial Facebook post and reach out to Leeya.

See the angels, Be the angels...

Message of the day

Who needs an angel visit today?

Day 32

SIBLINGS

I am an only child.

My husband is an only child.

We have 4 children.

We live in a constant state of ???

"Is it normal to _____ your sibling?"

Insert:

fight, prank, ignore, hate, annoy, fart on, steal from, trade with, tell on, lie for...

The list was endless.

And the sibling connection was perplexing.

Usually, just when Brian and I, speechless and scratching our heads, wondered how these two would ever get along, they walked back in and had already moved on, usually laughing.

To know someone that intimately and to love them for who they are, flaws and all, is the first gift of unconditional love you receive.

I asked Rachel and Jay, who were fighting when I wrote this (after spending an entire day inside due to frigid temps and general laziness)...

When you think about your relationship with your sibling, what comes to mind?

Jay: "Kinda mean, kinda nice. We help each other when you need help. They can be annoying and get on my nerves. But when I think about them, I think LOVE. I feel LOVE."

Rachel: "I love all my brothers. I like how honest and sweet they are about anything. I'm grateful they helped me be who I am today. Otherwise, I'd be too girly. My brothers have shaped me to be tough."

This sums up siblings. They shape you, they help you, they love you. It's not always perfect, but your life wouldn't be the same without them.

They each chose a bracelet for each other and danced around the room laughing. In the moment, they can drive each other crazy, but when they talk about the bigger picture, the relationship they have, they light up in love.

If you really want to recognize your sibling bond, order a bracelet for them and tell them what the relationship means to you.

That day, I spoke to Renoi in Kenya. She sent me all these bracelets from her village and she had lost her older sister two weeks ago, unexpectedly. When I shared my condolences this morning, she replied, "I really miss her. She was my very close friend."

Message of the day

Take a moment to appreciate your sibling...and tell them, so this only child, and everyone else, can all share the love.

Day 33

SERVICE

We all have so many things to be grateful for.

On this day, I chose to thank the firefighters of the world.

"Angels can't be everywhere, that is why God gave us firefighters."

The ones that run into danger, looking to protect, help and serve.

The Bend crew deserve to be at the top of the list!

Every time we have stopped by, they have had smiles on their faces, and taken time to visit. They took Tyler's pacifiers in 2006 when he had to quit and "donate them to another kid who needed them." They gave Rachel's Brownie Troop a tour in 2012. Last year we had to call on them more than a few times when my mom was having health issues. They are always calm, kind and compassionate.

On this day, they took time to hear about the Kenyan bracelets...and they all decided they were going to wear them and spread the love.

So if you are wondering if men can wear the bracelets too—THEY CAN!

These guys embodied the bracelet message of spreading love and kindness in our community.

Thank you, firefighters everywhere...we are forever GRATEFUL!

Message of the day

Thank someone who serves your community today!

Day 34

LIGHTWORKERS

I want to get this message right, because the bracelet that I gave with this story is symbolic of so much more.

Jessica is a therapist. A gifted, amazing child and adolescent therapist.

All day long, her chosen profession is to listen to someone's inner battle, with sacred attention, compassionate empathy, and wise problem-solving skills. She gently carries each person's heart for the time she is with them and then turns it around in a way that helps them see it for themselves.

Jessica has been an amazing resource for our family. There have been others before her at different stages of our life and I am thankful for each and every one of them.

The day after my Dad died, I called a therapist for the first time. I knew that I needed someone else to help me put the pieces of my broken heart back together again. I went every week for three years, and I can confidently say that I am a better version of myself having had someone walk with me through my grief and a complicated father-daughter relationship. I learned that it's natural to want to avoid the suffering we feel, to push it away, and move on. However, therapy taught me something powerful—not to be scared to look at the darkness inside, but that with the help of another, you can walk into it with awareness, wisdom, strength, and understanding.

This period of my life was a gift that prepared me for later. Parenting. I have had kids experience typical childhood ups and downs. However, I also have kids with anxiety and mental illness. If you have a child that suffers, you know that therapists and mental health professionals can literally be lifesavers. Having been prepared to walk through hard stuff by doing my own work, I was able to walk beside them with confidence and hope.

Sometimes our suffering prevents us from living our best life. The key is being brave enough to look inside at the dark and asking someone to help you see the light. That's why I call them lightworkers.

Lightworkers are therapists, counselors, life coaches, friends, parents, neighbors....any and everyone who is willing to hold your troubled heart for a bit and help you see the light.

After I thanked Jessica for the important work she does each day, for the appreciation for what she has done for our family, and for the amazing gift she has to help people along their journey, I gifted her the bracelet. She and I both got emotional. She explained that she couldn't accept gifts with monetary value, part of therapist rules, however we both agreed that she pick one and pay it forward. We decided she would choose someone, someone who needed to know that people cared about them, that they were part of a community who wanted them to know there is hope and they are loved. Jessica chose one that was red, white and blue. She said, "our country is so divided right now, but I want this to symbolize that we are all the same, connected by our humanity and hope."

I asked Jessica to sum up what she hoped all of her clients take away after working with her.

She said, "Suffering is something we all have in common. However, we all have different amounts of shame. If we have a lot of shame around the parts of ourselves we don't like, and we focus on these differences, we isolate ourselves. When we connect with someone and share, we realize our struggle is what actually unites us and makes us realize we are all alike. Things can get better and connection and community are what heals us." This bracelet gift is for any and everyone:

Who is a lightworker.

Who needs a lightworker.

Who is suffering.

Who is scared.

Who is sad.

Who is hurting.

Who is grieving.

Whose marriage is dark.

Whose children are struggling.

Who doesn't like themselves right now.

Who feels that mental illness makes you less-than.

CONNECT. YOU MATTER. YOU ARE LOVED. YOU CAN DO THIS. YOU ARE BEAUTIFUL. YOU ARE ENOUGH.

Message of the day

Someone out there might need to hear this today and know that they are not alone. Take them a bracelet and break the stigma!

Day 35

LET GO, LET IN

I tend to help a lot of people on street corners during this Power of Connection Challenge. That seems to be where those struggling plant themselves to make their needs most visible. They are easy to spot, which makes it easier to help.

However, on this day, I met a woman who has graced a street corner of Bend with another purpose over the years...to dance.

That's right Bendites: I was fortunate enough to meet Mary, the legendary Rock on,

Bend Little Ceasars lady!"

I reached out to Mary through her Facebook page. I'd seen a recent post that indicated she was having some health problems. I wanted to gift her a bracelet as a thank you for all the joy she has brought to our community over the years.

Her daughter responded to my message right away.

"That is very sweet of you! Please give her a call, I'm sure she'd be happy to hear from you. She's been having a very rough time and I unfortunately am not there to help her. Even just someone to talk to, I'm sure she'd appreciate. Thanks again for reaching out!"

I called Mary, someone I knew from around town, but a complete stranger up to this point. The phone rang several times and her machine picked up. I started leaving a long message and about halfway through, a voice picked up. "I'm here, this is Mary."

We proceeded to talk for half an hour. She told me all about her situation, there were tears, laughs and more tears. She was having back surgery in a few weeks and had to quit smoking in order to be approved by insurance. Chronic pain and changing a lifetime habit—she was in a rough spot. Dance was her medicine, something her body wasn't physically able to do anymore. I asked her if I could bring her a bracelet and anything else she might need. She said she would love the company, so I headed right over.

We sat in her apartment and talked like long lost friends. We talked and talked and talked. All I could think of was how sad it is that don't we make time for this type of visiting anymore. How many people are struggling from this lack of community?

Sometimes we get in our own way of connection. We agreed that the face we put on for others, the happy one you see dancing on the street corner, is often just a mask covering up the one at home struggling in silence. These are the people who aren't asking for help. They are struggling alone...and it's an intense battle, with no street sign for help. I told her Facebook was a lot like this. It looks great on the outside, but we rarely know how someone is doing on the inside.

I shared with her my mission with the bracelets. She was blown away. She picked out three. One for herself, one for her daughter and one to pay forward. We concluded that we need each other. Everyone needs someone. Women need to help women. We need to connect with our community. She loved the idea of the Kenyan women helping each other, working together.

Mary's eyes were teary, "I really want to help other women, and I need others to help me. The only problem is...asking for help, showing our weakness, admitting that we can't do it all alone, that scares me."

At the end of our visit, I asked Mary how she would sum up our conversation for this Facebook post. She looked at me with new tears in her eyes, "Let go and let in. I need to let go of my fears, judgement of myself, my sadness and grief and let in connection and help from others. This is the first time I have let go let in...well, maybe ever," she said.

"How does it feel Mary?" I asked.

"I'm so glad I answered the phone," she smiled.

Let go and Let in...

She picked up her guitar and lit up with a smile.

I asked Mary if she needed anything more, and she said, "Tell everyone to buy a Kenyan bracelet and if they need someone to sit with them during a hard time, cheer them on when they are quitting smoking, or just to talk, to call me."

I jumped up and yelled, "Mary look at you, you are already letting go and letting in!" and we laughed until we cried.

Message of the day

Who do you know that needs a visit? Take a bracelet and sit a bit with them. Don't struggle in silence—reach out, let go and let someone in. We all need each other.

Day 36

LET'S ALL GET ALONG

I got a call from my daughter today at lunch. She was in tears after some middle school friendship problems. I normally encourage her to work it out, let it go, or pop in to her school counselor for some extra support. However today sounded urgent. "Come get me—I can't stay here today, I need you." There was something in her voice and in my intuition that prompted me to go pick her up for some mother-daughter time.

We talked together as I ran some errands. Little bits of information, feelings, words said, choices made, slowly took shape. My heart aches for her as she is starting to navigate bigger life lessons, even though she is still a little girl.

As we started towards home, we passed a man sitting at the corner of the road. I rolled down the window and asked, "Hi! What do you need most?" He approached the car and with a twinkle in his eye and said, "I need everyone to put their guns down and stop fighting! I need everyone to stop fighting and just get along!" He turned around and started to walk back to his street corner. Rachel and I looked at each other-both confused about how to help.

So I said again, "But what do you need? Like right now?"

He smiled and said, "Oh, actually I would love some chili and a hot dog."

"Okay! We will be right back with that!" I chuckled at the simplicity and matter of fact-ness of his request.

We drove to nearby Sonic and ordered the footlong chili-covered hot dog. We returned to the corner and got out to bring our new friend his food.

We learned his name is John. He was born and raised here...a graduate of Bend High School.

I gifted John a bracelet and he eagerly let me place it on his wrist. It took some stretching to get it over his hand. He commented on how clean and bright it looked next to his "dirty hand." He said it made him feel new. I told him that it should remind him that he matters, that people care about him. He went on to tell us that all of his friends have passed away, most of them before they turned 30. He didn't think he would live as long as he has, turning 61 eleven days from then, to be exact.

As we left, Rachel and I both realized the important significance of John's original and very timely message: "Put down the guns and stop fighting!" That's what we all need most today and always is to focus on our connections and not our differences, value our friendships and "just get along."

Message of the day

Who needs a message of peace today?

SMILE

I stopped and talked with Jackie because of her sign. She sat on the busy corner holding her sign with a huge smile on her face. I watched as a steady stream of cars passed by while she grinned from ear to ear.

I often have people tell me "you are always smiling"...and I usually am. I actually think God decided to put me on this Earth to offer my smiles to people on a daily basis. So naturally I was drawn to this other smiler.

I walked up to Jackie and said, "What do you need most today?"

She replied, "Oh, anything, actually."

"But what do you need MOST?", I nudged.

"Well, we were given groceries already, so we have been blessed."

I told her, "I want to give you a special bracelet." So I picked one out and she squealed. "I love it, I love it, I LOVE IT." I told her that I wanted her to know that I care about her and want her to be reminded that she matters. She smiled. She put it on. I noticed her tattoo.: "MOM". I asked her about it, and she said yes, it's what defines her. Then she looked up and said, "Actually, I know something I would love."

"What?" I asked.

"I would love to take my boy to the movies. You know, something normal, like that."

So I picked up two movie passes and brought them back to her. She smiled, I smiled, and we parted.

Two smiling moms...now forever connected.

Update: A friend bumped into Jackie 6 months later and when she commented on her bracelet, Jackie replied in a video to me, "You gave me this bracelet. I wanted to tell you that your smile made my day, made my week and you made a lot of difference in my life. I just want to thank you. I wear it every day and never take it off, shower and everything. So thank you!"

"Peace begins with a smile." —Mother Teresa

Message of the day

Who needs a smile to make their day today and a bracelet to remember it by?

Day 38

HOPE

When my son's close friend Deshaun passed away, I was crippled with grief. And fear. And shock.

I was speechless and paralyzed.

We all tried to make sense of something that could not be reasoned or explained away.

As I grappled with the sad reality, I remembered that compassion means we struggle together. To me that meant I needed to show up, in whatever way the family needed. I reached out and connected with a pastor and his wife that were with the family. They provided a link for support. They also signed me up for a meal on Sunday and gave me a Christmas list for the family.

Then the beautiful story of compassion unfolded. Of a community struggling together. People stepped up to help, asked for ways to support, and bought a Christmas tree and presents for the kids. My very first friend in Bend, who has weathered all of life's storms with me, asked to join me in shopping for the meal and delivering it. The community rallied to raise funds for funeral expenses. People sent poems and letters, food and prayers.

Barack Obama states, "The best way to not feel hopeless is to get up and do something. Don't wait for good things to happen to you. If you go out and make some good things happen, you will fill the world with hope, you will fill yourself with hope."

Sunday came and we did our shopping. We found soft blankets for the little brothers and a hoodie for the oldest. We bought movie tickets, and food. Lots of food.

As we drove to the apartment, the car was quiet. My friend said, "This is what we do. We show up even when it's hard. We don't wait and wonder. We show up."

As we parked and headed to the apartment, Deshaun's father Donavan stood outside on the phone. He ended the call and wiped away his tears. He invited us in.

He was home with his youngest two boys. His wife and oldest boy were out shopping for clothes for the service.

We set down the food and played with the 6-year-old they affectionately call Bubbas. He was drawn to the soft blanket we brought with wide eyes and a smile. His little brother Noah was asleep on the couch, tired from a very long day at church.

The four of us sat on the floor. Bubbas gave hugs and looked at us curiously. We told Donavan that we were here for their family and that everyone was thinking of them and sending prayers and love. Donavan said thank you, he said their family felt a huge outpouring of support from the community. "It's overwhelming," he said.

I had reluctantly brought my bag of bracelets, not knowing if it would be the right time to explain my mission. Instead, I just sat the bag down on the floor. "Bubbas," I said, "do you want a bracelet? I think I have the perfect one for you." I fished around in the bag and found a small bracelet. He put out his arm and we stretched it over his hand. He was so excited. He dug through the bag some more. "Pick out another for your little brother," we said. He spent time looking for one that would fit. At this point, we told Donavan that he should pick one. As he tried on different styles, I explained that each bracelet was given to someone special. It is a symbol that we are all connected. That you are not alone. Donavan shook his head in understanding. He smiled. He found a bracelet and put it on. He picked out a bracelet for his oldest son. Then we asked Bubbas to pick out a bracelet for his mama. He picked out several, but nothing seemed perfect. Suddenly a brass bracelet appeared, with blue beads. Donavan said, "That's the one for mama. A blue bracelet to represent all of her boys."

Yes, we all agreed in unison. All of her boys. And a reminder that our entire community supported and loved them.

We all hugged and told them we would continue checking in. And then we left.

And we were filled with a little more hope than when we came.

Message of the day

Who needs your support to provide hope today?

Day 39

SELF LOVE

It is said that, "To love others you must first love yourself." Do you love yourself?

I heard a disturbing statistic the other day.

When asked, "Do you like the way you look?" the vast majority (like almost 100%) responded NO.

This is a big problem. We are SO HARD ON OURSELVES.

Now ask almost any child that question and they almost inevitably answer YES! I love myself! I am amazing! I am beautiful!

Where do we lose the idea of loving ourselves?

I think the answer in part is that as adults, we focus on the negative, the lack, the mistakes, the disappointments. We focus on the "never good enough" physical appearance that society floods us with.

We have forgotten to be in connection with our essence, our core, and our unique spirit.

SO—

I encourage you to find a picture of yourself from childhood that captures your true essence, before "life" started to shape you.

Ask yourself, What do you see when you look at her? (or him)

For me, I see love, light, joy, goodness.

THIS IS YOU. THIS IS WHO YOU ARE.

Looking at your picture, Would you ever tell that child that one day she will be unattractive?

That she won't accomplish her dreams.

That she won't be loved.

That she won't matter.

That she will be a disappointment.

HECK NO you wouldn't. So why would you say that to yourself now? Or think it? Why do you put yourself down? Why do you judge yourself? Why do you think you aren't good enough? Why do you think you are unattractive?

I challenge you to find a picture of yourself as a child and post it somewhere you will see it every day.

I hope seeing your childhood self will inspire you to smile back and connect to your true essence once again.

And you will remember that YOU ARE BEAUTIFUL SIMPLY BECAUSE YOU ARE YOU!

Message of the day

Gift a bracelet to yourself and remember who you are at your core.

Day 40

BABY GIRL

To my baby girl...These pictures are of us at the same age.

Both fresh from a day of sun and swimming at the pool. Relaxed in our beanbags. I, with a half-eaten cookie and my stuffed animal companions, and you with your powdered-donut-covered lips.

The end of a well lived, perfect summer day.

Fast forward to today and soon you will turn 13.

Here's the thing...I have so much to share about what I have learned in my own 44 years of life experience.

And my gut instinct every time is to try and protect you

I want you to only see the good. To soar and thrive and never have a bad day.

It's natural I think. To want the best for you.

So I push, overstep, overbear, or overreact, thinking that somehow I can CONTROL what happens and I can PREVENT you from making that mistake, getting hurt or struggling.

But here's the thing.

With every mistake, hurt, struggle, and challenge that entered my life, I have grown, survived, and thrived.

Every day gives me new opportunities to try, try harder, love and love some more.

I am a stronger, softer, gentler, kinder, wiser, and no doubt better version of myself.

Life, made up of all those up and down days, has shaped the girl in the beanbag into ME.

Now because you are uniquely YOU, your life will take its own winding path.

And I will cheer the loudest, listen the hardest and support you unconditionally, whenever you need me.

But the two things I want you to carry with you along every step of your path are knowing that you are perfect and that you are loved.

Mistakes, disappointments, struggle and hurt will happen. I don't have to shield you from it anymore, because I know you too will find your own strength and your own resilience and your own solutions. You will grow, survive, thrive and more.

And all of this will lead you to countless moments when you are overwhelmed with GRATITUDE for a day well spent outside in the sun, where you rest and realize, that your one AMAZING life is PERFECTLY well lived and is all yours.

May you wear this bracelet to remind you: I love you baby girl.

Message of the day

Who needs the reminder that their one AMAZING life is PERFECTLY well lived?

Day 41

LUCK AND LUIGI

Friday the 13th is superstitiously unlucky and yesterday proved no exception. So I shook it off and turned that luck around today by following my mantra that the more we give the better we feel.

Evan was sitting on the corner with a sign that read: Homeless, Anything Helps.

I stopped and walked over to talk to him. "How can I help you most?" I said as I greeted him. He tried his hardest to stand up but he was stiff and slow. Luigi, his beautiful

Great Dane, came over to warm up by me, shivering. Once he was able to stand, he replied that he needed "dog food and maybe some food for myself."

He told me his name was Evan and he lived on Dirt Hill, a place nearby where a group of people live outside.

We chatted for a bit about his day and then I told him about my project. I told him that every day this month I chose someone to help and that today it was him. As we talked a woman came up from the Humane Society and gave Luigi a coat, a blanket and some food.

In that moment I realized how easy it is to know how to help homeless pets—food and warmth. Maybe it feels intimidating to ask a homeless person what they need because their answer may be more unpredictable?

So I asked again, "Evan, if you could make a list about what YOU really need, I will work on it and see what I can get to help."

He looked at me with surprise and said, "Well then. I guess I really need a tent, mine is really old and torn. And a cot—you saw how hard it is for me to get up from the ground. And gloves. Boots (8.5). Really anything to stay warm. Oh and a bike. With a trailer…that would be amazing. It's hard for me to walk with my condition and a bike would make things so much easier."

He told me about his girlfriend Sam and his extensive comic book collection. "Reading comic books is my favorite form of entertainment," he said with a big smile. "If anyone has extra comic books I would love to read them."

I pictured Evan and Luigi in their tent reading comic books and it made me happy. Simple pleasures and humble requests—this is what Christmas is really about.

We arranged a way to get in touch and I gave him two bracelets—one for himself and one for Sam.

When I first asked what he needed most, Evan said food. However when I told him that I wanted to help, he opened up and told me what he REALLY needed. A Home. Warmth.

Transportation .

This is such a good reminder in life. True and meaningful connection creates trust. And when we trust, we can say what we really need.

In a matter of days, I was able to help Evan get some essentials to stay warm this winter. I collected a tent, a cot, size large gloves, a warm hat, a Safeway card, a bike trailer, bike, and boots. One friend made a tray of homemade mac and cheese. We even obtained a donated Christmas tree that Evan proudly displayed and decorated for the camp.

Oh...and comic books.

This is The Power of Connection Project.

We are stronger together.

Love one another.

Give more.

Stay humble.

Laugh.

Message of the day

Make it your mission to spark a deeper conversation and ask someone what they REALLY need.

Day 42

MAMAS

Today is all about moms.

A friend last week asked if I knew of anyone who could use some boy hand me downs. She had recently cleaned out closets and wanted to share the goods with someone who could use it. So I picked up the load and delivered it today to two mamas who are neighbors and share just about everything with each other to help each other out. They pass things over the fence, encourage and support each other. The way a village should be.

As I delivered the load, I connected with a mama on Facebook who was discouraged. She couldn't afford diapers for her baby, having used the last of her money for gas. I reached out and asked her what she needed most. She told me diapers and vitamins. So I headed to the store to do my own grocery shopping and picked up the items she requested. I sent her one last message, "I am at the store...anything else you might need?" She responded with two more requests: Milk for her son and almond milk for herself. I added those to my cart and headed to deliver the groceries.

I arrived at her apartment and dropped off the items. She was incredibly grateful. Her name was Logan and I gave her a bracelet and explained the project. We chatted about her life and she blew me away with her story. She had previously been in jail and was now on the last days of her parole. She was 14 months sober! She was encouraged to get an abortion when she got pregnant, but chose to get clean and be a mama to her son. She had her baby and got help at Grandma's House. This was a mama who has suffered through postpartum depression. Now she was in her own place and researched vitamins for her baby and showed me her collection of HOMEMADE baby food in the freezer. She was kind, loving and beautiful. Recently, she had an experience of "Mom-shaming" at her church that she attends every Sunday. This really upset her. It upsets me too. I cannot think of a more shining example of redemption, grace and love, than this woman.

Then the coolest thing happened. I told her that another mama, Jennifer, had given me a book to gift to another person I met during this challenge. Without knowing anything about her, I brought the book with me to give Logan as a gift. It is all about the meaning of Christmas and specifically, HOPE. It is from a mama who had also been through a hard time.

Logan took me over and showed me the Bible that she carried in her purse. It was the one she was given in jail. It was taped and falling apart, but full of the details of her hard work and perseverance to get to this day, healthy and strong.

Thank you for the reminder today, Logan, that vulnerability is what connects us. That when we ask for help and share our stories, we learn from and inspire each other to be better.

As I left we hugged at least 10 times.

She seemed to want the hug for validation and strength. I equally wanted the hug for the same reasons.

She cried. As I left and walked to my car I cried too.

I am in awe.

How can anyone shame this mama or any mama.

No one is perfect. No one knows what road we all have walked to get to today.

Stop judging, start loving.

We all need our village.

Mamas helping mamas.

Mamas lifting, encouraging, supporting and sharing.

Shout out to all the mamas (and the ones who are watching over us).

Oh, and get this! Logan knows Evan, from yesterday's post. When she got out of jail, she had nothing and lived in the woods with...you guessed it...Evan and his friends! She plans to go with me to deliver the items we collected.

I am incredibly inspired by you Logan! XOXO

Message of the day

Stop judging, start hugging. Find someone today who needs strength
and validation and give them a hug, and maybe a bracelet!

Day 43

EVERY DAY

Today I had to run into Walgreen's to grab a quick item.

As I stood in line I realized that there was a problem with the cashier and the card reader. The cashier, Rose, wanted to make sure the customer was getting his reward points and the computer system was not cooperating. She tried, tried and tried again. Every time she had him re-enter his information, it failed again. He was not kind about the problem. He was actually quite rude. He slammed his bag of items on the counter and stormed out.

Rose, looking startled (and tired), quietly slid the bag to the side, and greeted me with a smile.

She scanned my two items and had me enter my information. Fail. Re-enter, Fail. Again. Fail. Re-enter, Fail. Again. I touched Rose on the hand and said, "Rose, I appreciate your patience and how hard you are trying to make this work. But it's okay, let's just skip that part. Okay?"

We finished the transaction and she gave me my receipt. "Keep this receipt honey and you can go online and get your points. There is also a survey where you can rate my service."

I told Rose that I would definitely take the survey and that I would give her the highest rating. She smiled. Then I took the bracelet off my wrist and put it on Rose. I told her about the women in Kenya and the Power of Connection project. She said she had never seen such a beautiful piece of jewelry. Then I asked, "Rose, what is your Christmas Wish this year?"

She took a deep breath and said, "My only wish is for good health, peace and love. And to thank God every day. Every day. Every day." With each "every day," Rose pounded her hands on the counter for emphasis. With the last "every day," she leaned closer to my face and emphasized the words so that she was sure that I understood. I nodded in agreement.

I hear you loud and clear, Rose.

Good Health.

Peace.

Love.

Gratitude.

Christmastime can feel like a rush to complete all the tasks. To get it all done. To get all the right gifts. It can feel material and stressful.

However, some people are struggling at Christmas.

In the last two weeks I have personally spent time with people who are:

*battling chronic health problems

*fighting cancer

*suffering mental health issues, either themselves or their children

*battling alcoholism or are newly sober

*experiencing a divorce, a separation, or a first Christmas alone

*working through traumatic memories of loss at Christmas

* frustrated

*stressed

*anxious

*sad

*hopeless

*homeless

Remember Rose.

When life treats you harshly, seek gratitude.

Seek joy. Seek peace. Seek love.

Every day. Every day. Every day.

Reach out. Share your story. Listen. Love one another. Encourage. Support.

You are not alone.

This is the message that we need to hold onto and let ground us for the holidays.

We are stronger together.

This is The Power of Connection.

List all that you are grateful for and give thanks today. Every day. Every Day.

Day 44

BABIES

I had the amazing opportunity to watch a friend's baby boy today while she and her husband took their daughter to see her first movie, Frozen 2. I was so happy and honored that she took me up on my offer to babysit. Not only do I love the idea of helping a mom have some time off, but I LOVE baby snuggles. So often we don't allow each other to help. For whatever reason we don't ask when we really need it, or we have a hard time receiving it when it is offered. I have learned that life is best lived with a village of support.

As I left my new buddy, I asked this friend if she could use some fluffy kids Pottery Barn Beanbag Chairs that I had in my trunk for Goodwill. She didn't have room for them, so I headed out to pick up my own 13-year-old baby girl from school. She had horseback riding lessons today and as we loaded her things, my 16-year-old son Tyler asked to ride with me to drop her off. We headed to the barn and I thought to myself how thankful I have been to have so many people in my life who I trust with my babies. Grandparents, babysitters, teachers, coaches, musicians and youth group leaders, have all poured their gifts into my children and made meaningful connections. When I don't have all the answers, my kids and I can lean on the village for support.

After we dropped Rachel off we headed to drop the chairs at Goodwill. When I arrived, they said they can't take "beanbag chairs." The chairs, filling the back of the car, needed to find a home. As we pulled out of the parking lot, I noticed a young man sitting on the corner playing his guitar. We pulled up and rolled down the window. "Hi, how are you? Do you need something?" He replied, "Yes, ma'am. I really need some clothes. I am so cold. Maybe a heater?"

We were parked in front of Sportsman's Warehouse, so I asked if he wanted to go in and show me what he needed.

"Yes ma'am, that would be wonderful. I'm Jason." We put his backpack and guitar in my trunk and went in to shop. We looked at heaters, socks, thermals, tarps, pocketknives and propane, but he scoffed at every price tag. "This is too expensive. No way. Too much. I would never want you to pay that."

We settled on him letting me buy a headlamp for $15.99.

"I have to walk 11 miles to my shelter and the shoes I am wearing are too small. My bike and trailer were stolen. My phone too. I have nothing," Jason said. "I am really, really cold."

My friend had just donated an extra bike to me. "I have a bike for you!" He looked shocked and broke down crying. "I was praying when you pulled up. I was praying. God sure works fast."

I gave him his things out of my trunk and when he saw the chairs, his eyes fixated on them. "You are welcome to have them," I said. His eyes watered again. "My little sister is homeless too. I have to bring her these. She will be so happy." I told him I could go grab the bike. I rushed home and loaded the bike, grabbed an extra pair of old size 13 Nikes, and some hand warmers. I rushed back. When I unloaded the bike he sank to his knees crying. "I have never had a bike this nice in my whole life. It even has a kickstand."

He was speechless and completely overcome with gratitude. He told us that he was a straight A student and graduated high school. He lost a friend to suicide last month. My son said he, too, lost a friend and they shared their grief. Jason said, "You don't lose people, you gain angels." As we drove off, Jason sat on the ground next to his new bike and put his face in his hands, his shoulders jerking up and down through sobs.

Jason needs a village.

This is someone's baby that I helped tonight.

Who knows how he arrived here at this moment, but he and his baby sister are homeless and I know his mom would want us to take care of her babies.

This is The Power of Connection Project.

Message of the day

Think about gifting something you aren't using anymore to someone in need. You may just provide the hope someone needs and change someone's life for the better.

Day 45

SHARING

I met up with Jason again this morning to deliver the items that I collected over the last two days. It was a HUGE load that included: bike trailers, tire pump, bike lock, socks, gloves, backpack, water jug, pocket knives, propane, propane heater, rope, tarps, jacket, old Iphone and charger, hand warmers, sleeping bag, sleeping pad, flashlights, food, and more. He was blown away. Thanks to each and every person who contributed, it was truly amazing!

Luckily his friend Daryl was there with his van because they planned to take Jason to turn in his cans for money. When Daryl saw the huge load, he offered to pack it in his van and drive Jason the 11 miles to camp. Mind you, Daryl's van is his home. He has a bed in the center and only the space in the back holds his few possessions. Well, we all started shoving trailers, bike and supplies in the van and Daryl couldn't have been nicer about us cluttering up his home.

Jason explained that Daryl is like a second father to him. Daryl agreed, and said that he "loved Jason as if he were his own son." He said he would do anything for him.

I said to Daryl, "Your kindness is incredible. What do you need that I can try and help with?" He replied that he didn't need anything, he just liked taking care of other people.

Jason said he was going to take Daryl to lunch with his pop can money to thank him. He also said he was going to share his supplies with so many others out there that need help, too. "I can help a lot of people with this," he said with a big hug.

The amazing thing about this huge load of love was that 99% of the items CAME FROM YOUR HOMES. All the amazing people that came together to make this happen shared something of theirs to help Jason. And Jason wants to share it too.

Message of the day

Helen Keller said, " Alone, we can do so little; together we can do so much."
Can you gather a group of people to make a collective difference for someone?
We are stronger TOGETHER.

Day 46

THANK YOU!

Sometimes I give a bracelet just to say thank you.

A few days ago, my post was about babies.

Well today I had my annual appointment with the doctor who delivered two of mine.

I can't think of anyone who embodies compassion, kindness, connection and love like Dr. John Murphy.

He sees women at their most vulnerable and is calm, caring and incredibly reassuring. He laughs, cries, worries and celebrates with each and every patient. He truly cares.

I gave him his bracelet and told him how much I appreciated him. I told him that he is kind, empathetic and compassionate and that is what these bracelets symbolize for me. He gave me a huge hug and said how much that meant to him. Then he said he was worried he wouldn't be able to get it over his huge hand.

Those hands bring new babies into the world every day. Those hands ease the worries of new and expecting moms. Those hands console parents. Those hands clap and cheer. Those hands are healing. Those hands are gifts.

He pulled that bracelet right onto and over his "huge" hand and he smiled. "It's never coming off now!"

As I left the office the staff were all asking how they could buy a bracelet too.

Message of the day

Girls in Kenya often end up pregnant at 13 if they don't continue their schooling. With the purchase of this book, you had a hand in changing that for a Kenyan girl. Thank you!

Day 47

GRIEF

Georgia is a sweet angel dog tonight.

We were told this afternoon that she had an aggressive form of lymphoma. She died in our arms with all of us rubbing her and telling her how much we loved her.

Grief is complicated.

The day after my Dad died 9 years ago, I called a breeder in Georgia and asked her if she had any puppies. She said she had one girl, and that puppy was on a plane to Oregon the next day. Georgia loved each of us so well.

Dogs give us unlimited love and expect nothing in return.

We can all learn from that.

The vet who assisted us with Georgia was amazing. As he sat with us and listened to our sobs, I looked at him and said how hard it must be to do this for so many families. He started to cry and excused himself from the room. When he came back, he said, "She knew she was surrounded by love. That is what is important. That's what we all want."

I gave him a bracelet that was made of a variety of colors.

I imagine that each bead represents someone's grief. A pet. A parent. A child. A spouse. A friend.

This vet helped to ease our pain. Like a rainbow after the storm, I gave him a rainbow bracelet. May he always remember how many lives, pets and people he has so lovingly touched.

We all experience grief.

When Georgia arrived in my arms, I was broken. I truly believe my Dad sent her to me for comfort, protection, companionship and healing. She never failed to provide all of the above and more. She was perfect. When she left me today, I didn't know how I was going to do life without her.

But I know my answer to grief.

Connection. Love. More love. Selfless love. Angels. And rainbows.

Thank you for your love and support. Heaven is brighter and covered with lots of new dog hair tonight.

Message of the day

Grief is not meant to do alone. How can you connect with someone who might need your love today to help ease their loss?

Day 48

BE AN ENCOURAGER

This challenge started as an answer to my own bout with loneliness and finding my way four years ago.

What I have learned in the last three years, without a doubt, is that everyone needs meaningful connections. And meaningful connections can happen every day, in many ways.

The first Sunday of every month I serve breakfast to the homeless at the Salvation

Army. Miriam and I have seen each other every month for the last year. However, I never sat down and chatted with her until today.

Connections often start with small talk.

She is a 30-year breast cancer survivor.

She lives alone in a mobile home after her husband left her several years ago.

She has no income and is barely able to pay her water bill.

She is living off "soda cans," as she puts it—using the $10 she gets for redeeming them each day for gas.

She has a 1990 Jeep (with no power steering) that she uses to get to the soup kitchen each day for meals. This is her only source of food.

She stays warm in her home by keeping a fire going with wood for her heat. She wears 4 down jackets all the time.

She's a mom and grandmother.

I told her about the Power of Connection Project.

I told her I started it because I needed to challenge myself to connect more. To ask for help and support when I needed it.

Then I told her that I wanted to help her.

She simply started crying. I held her hand and listened attentively.

"No one wants to ask for help. No one wants to admit that they can't handle their own shit. But I need help. I'm barely making it. I am grateful to you just for saying that you want to help. I don't even care about anything else. Just saying you want to help makes me cry. I can't ask my kids. It's the last thing a parent should ever have to do."

I asked her what her Christmas wish was.

She said her car is the most important thing, because it gets her out of the house and gets her to food. However, it needs power steering and money for gas.

Then she got really quiet.

"I also wish I could go back and thank my husband for everything. I took him for granted. Now that he's gone, I realize how much he really did for me. He was a good man. I wish I could say thank you and I'm sorry. It's so hard to do life alone."

I listened. We hugged. I gave her a bracelet and we hugged some more.

She told me the bracelet was so "encouraging."

I told her we all could use more encouraging. I thanked her for sharing her story with me and allowing me to encourage her.

That can only happen from a meaningful connection.

I gave her $100 and told her it comes from a community of encouragers. She sobbed.

This is the Power of Connection Project.

Message of the day

Who can you encourage today?

Day 49:

CHRISTMAS WISH

December can feel like the month of constant errands. People often ask how I have time to do this challenge during such a busy season. But a meaningful connection can happen anytime, anywhere, in as little as 15 minutes of your day, if you are looking for it.

Tonight, I had to run to Safeway because my children stole all of the toilet paper. We looked under every sink and in every drawer. They had slowly been snatching it from each other's rooms and no one bothered to tell me that we were completely out. So of course, no toilet paper in the house = crisis. I braved the icy roads and headed to Safeway feeling annoyed.

As I walked into the store, I passed by the Salvation Army bell ringer. We said hello and exchanged smiles. I headed to the toilet paper aisle and then to the checkout, 6 people deep and moving slowly. I passed the time people watching. No one looked very happy.

As I made my way back outside, I decided to spend a few minutes with the bell ringer. He was really excited to talk. He told me his name was Steven and he had been a bell ringer for 7 years. I asked why he didn't come to breakfast at the Salvation Army and he said it was too far across town. He told me that his bike was stolen and he could only walk so far. He told me how bad the drivers are in the winter and I griped to him about my toilet paper problem. I really enjoyed Steven's company. He was gentle, kind and funny.

I told Steven that every day of December I choose one person to connect with and give a bracelet to. I told him that I wanted to choose him because he was so friendly, and I was really happy to see a friendly face. We found a bracelet that fit him and then I asked him, "What is your Christmas wish, Steven?" He looked startled.

He smiled and really gave it some thought. He started to say something a few times and then hesitated.

"Anything at all," I said. "What do you need most?"

He looked sure now. "I really need thermals. Like a good quality top and bottom. I am a men's 2XL. That is what I need. That would be the absolute best."

This is when I came to find out that Steven lives in the woods 5 miles from this bell ringing spot. He walks home to his tent and blankets at 7 p.m. each night. I learned that the Salvation Army hires the homeless to ring the bells and pays them by the hour. He is proud of his 7-year track record and that the director trusts him with such an important job.

I assured Steven that I would bring him some thermals tomorrow. But I couldn't help but wonder if we could grant him an even bigger Christmas wish?

A 26- or 27.5-inch mountain bike with a big red bow? Steven could get to work AND across town to the soup kitchen for meals.

This is the Power of Connection. Talking, sharing, caring. People helping people. It only took 15 minutes out of my day and I promise you that my toilet paper annoyance has long disappeared and is replaced by something so much bigger and better—LOVE.

Message of the day

Take the time to learn the story of the local bell ringer during the Holidays. Share it with your community and see what happens!

LISTEN

When we help others, we feel better.

It's the way our brains are wired.

Generosity triggers happiness in our brain.

You all showed such amazing care and generosity to me during my grief. You listened to my story and you honored my feelings about love and loss. Your kindness made me feel better and hopefully you felt better too. Connecting to someone else actually meets our most basic need—to relate to someone in a meaningful way.

I spent the day at home with an open door to friends and bracelet shoppers. I appreciated being surrounded by love both here in Bend and through Facebook.

Then I thought about Miriam and Steven, both living in the woods, alone and struggling.

I went to the auto parts store and bought the parts for Miriam's car. Her son has agreed to install them tomorrow. When I told Miriam the news, she said, "Kindness is love at its best."

Then I drove by to deliver Steven his thermals and a warm shirt I picked up at Costco. I also got to tell him the exciting news that someone is gifting him with a bike. He was so grateful. But Steven really just wanted to talk. So I gave him my time. For half an hour I just listened as he told me more about his life.

What excites him: The bands the Moody Blues and The Cure, playing the guitar, listening to Bible radio all evening until he goes to bed at 10, and studying Sociology.

I was patient and attentive. I honored his story.

Just like you all did for me.

We both felt better.

A little less lonely. Happier. Connected.

Listen to Steven on his Youtube channel if you have a minute. It's his band's name: YKANTIBU. He's playing a classical piece that made me happy.

Maybe listening more is the key to finding more joy.

Cheering each other on. Honoring stories. Giving.

I hope Steven and Miriam feel joy tonight. I know I do.

Message of the day

Thank you for reading along with these stories and listening to the details of my project.
We are forever connected and for that I am forever grateful. May you find joy, connection and love each and every day.
XOXO

Conclusion

Thanks to all of you who have supported this challenge by purchasing this book and sending Kenyan girls to school.

If you would like to purchase Kenyan bracelets, visit thepowerofconnectionproject.com.

My hope is that you have finished this book with a greater sense of connection to yourself, your family and your community.

May we all continue to connect more and love most—TOGETHER.

XOXO,

Andrea

About the Author

Andrea Rosenzweig is on a mission to help others discover the "Power of Connection." Over the last five years, she's been rallying her community to make a difference in the lives of others and has discovered that we are STRONGER TOGETHER.

It all started with a 24-day challenge during the month of December in 2016. Every year, Andrea purchases 24 pieces of socially conscious jewelry that are handmade in Kenya and gives them to random strangers every day leading up to Christmas with the goal of making a meaningful connection with someone new. It has since rippled into a larger movement, one that calls on people to make a positive impact by doing acts of good and connecting with others.

Andrea lives in Bend, Oregon with her husband and four beautiful children. While Bend is where they call home, they are still Southerners at heart, after living in Atlanta before moving to the West Coast 16 years ago. Andrea and her husband Brian are small business owners, operating an orthodontics practice, and they love spending time with their family and community. In the winter, they can usually be found cheering their kids on at various activities or lounging at home by the fire. In the summer, you'll find them at the pool, floating the river, or boating on Lake Billy Chinook.

Andrea was nominated for the Bend Chamber Woman of the Year, Community Hero Award in 2020 for her work with the Power of Connection project.

CPSIA information can be obtained
at www.ICGtesting.com
Printed in the USA
JSHW040841261121
20637JS00006BA/23